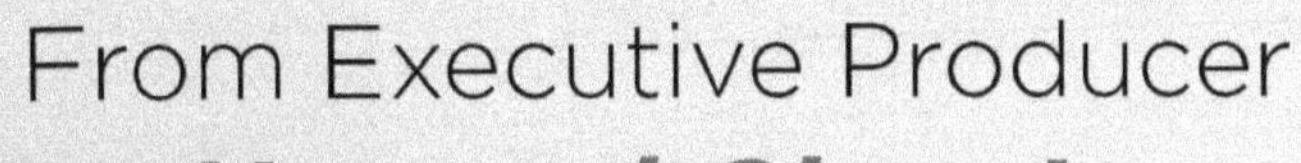

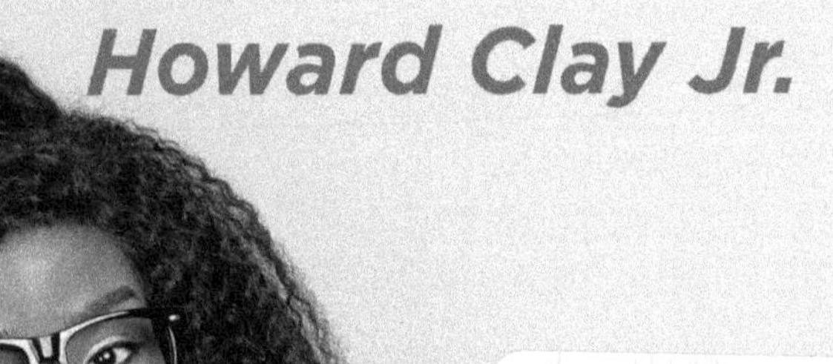

How to WRITE your TV Show/Movie in 31 days!

A COMPREHENSIVE GUIDE TO TRANSFORMING YOUR IDEA INTO A SCRIPT

How to Write a Tv/Movie Script in 31 Days!

written by

Howard Clay Jr.

Special thanks to my wife,
Suga Bear,
Love you with all my heart.

INTRO

First and foremost, I'd like to tell you, "thank you" for purchasing this book. It really means a lot to me and my ultimate mission of empowering new filmmakers to hone their craft and show up to tell their stories.
Of course, I believe a "congratulations" is in order for you and your decision to move towards your goal of writing a script!

Okay. Now that formalities are out of the way, let's get started.
I know exactly what you're thinking right now... "31 DAYS?! I can't write a script in 31 days!"

Trust me, I understand that bewildered look on your face because normally it can take around 60 to 90 days to formulate and write a rough draft. But, I believe after you read this book you will be able to complete a rough draft of a television pilot or a feature-length screenplay in 31 days…
Yes. Even if you've never written a

script before! That's right. I said it and I mean it… I truly believe this is possible.

I understand this may not apply to everyone, but another reason you may have decided to purchase this book is because you have a great idea, but you do not have the money to spend on hiring a writer to draft the script for you. This is a very legitimate reason for you to pick up this book.
So, regardless of whether it takes you 31 days or 90 days, this book is about to save you thousands of dollars and lots of time and frustration by teaching you the simplest ways to complete your first draft.

For us to better understand what we're actually doing, we have to define what a script is. According to vocabulary.com, "a script is a written

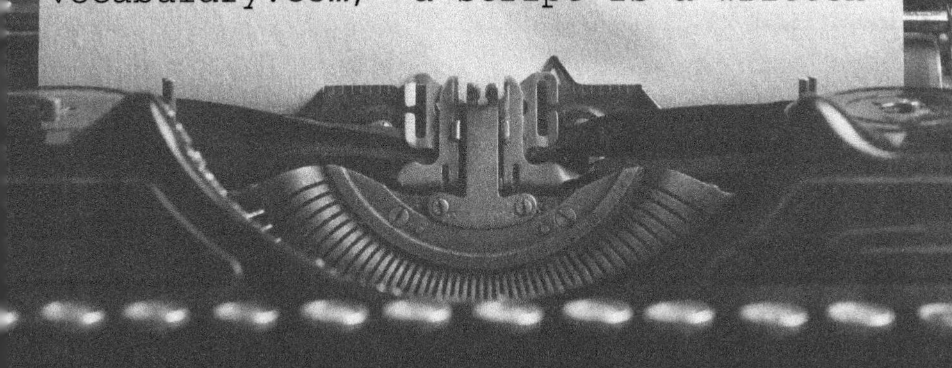

version of a play or movie." Seems simple enough, right?

The formal definition of a script is one thing to mull over, but let me tell you my opinion of a script. A script is ultimately a story written in a language filmmakers (cast and crew) can read, understand, and execute. With that being said, you may be a little confused, but you will understand exactly what this actually means when you are done with this book. Everyone has a story… literally. This is one of the first things I hear or one of the first questions people ask when they meet me and find out what I do.

"Can I tell you my story?"

So, yes. Everyone has a story. Your lived experience is a story. What comes from your imagination is a story. The convergence of others' experiences from your perspective is a story. Several things need to happen for these stories to become a script and that is where this book comes in.

We're going to go over a LOT in this book. Whether you're a 5-year writing vet or you're just getting started, some of this information will be new, and some of this information will be old. But at the end of this journey, you will have the knowledge needed to accomplish your goals. So again, thank you for picking up this book, and let's begin (or continue) the journey of you becoming a screenwriter… together.

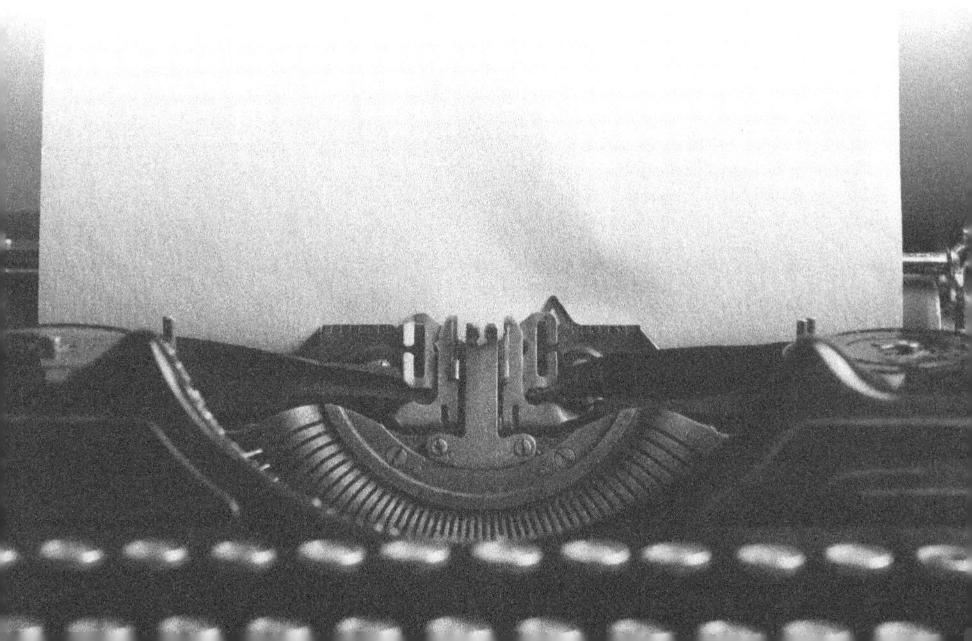

FADE IN.

CHAPTER 1
HOW DO I WRITE A SCRIPT?

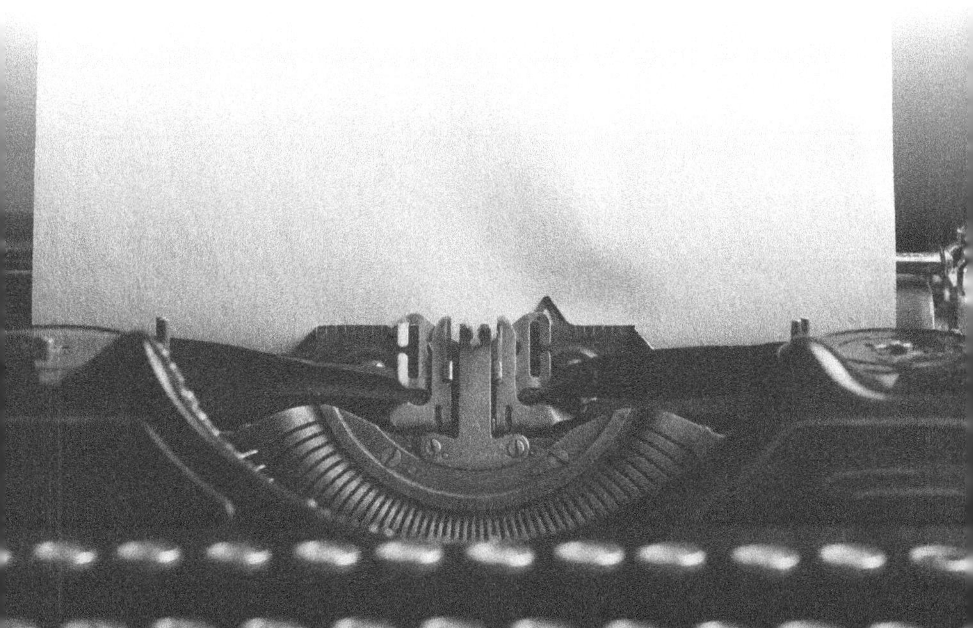

Writing a script is not rocket science, but there is a science to writing a script. I never learned about writing a script in any formal manner. I never took any classes, nor enrolled in any programs or seminars - nothing of the sort. But somehow I've managed to write - and shoot - a great number of film and television scripts.

Let me take you back to where it all began for me because I believe it is a very important story to tell. So, let's start at the beginning.

The year was 2002. (I accept that some of you weren't even born yet and that's okay.) It was 2002 and I was working full-time at a University after recently finishing college with a major in sociology and a minor in religion. I had been married to my first wife for about a year at this point and everything was going seemingly great with my career as well as my marriage. I was excited about my future at the University and also excited about my future with a lot of projects I began

in Cincinnati. But one day I woke up
with a story in my head.

Let me explain.

The University choir, which I was in
charge of, had just come back from
being on tour performing at several
HBCUs (Historically Black Colleges and
Universities). It was an amazing trip
and we learned a lot about HBCUs and
their heritage. One of the schools we
visited was Fisk University.

Nothing special happened on the trip
and I promise I didn't hit my head.
However, one day, one very regular
morning, I woke up with a story in
my mind that I couldn't get rid of.
I could literally see all of the
characters, the scenes, storylines,
all as if I were watching a movie. I
went about as normal as possible for

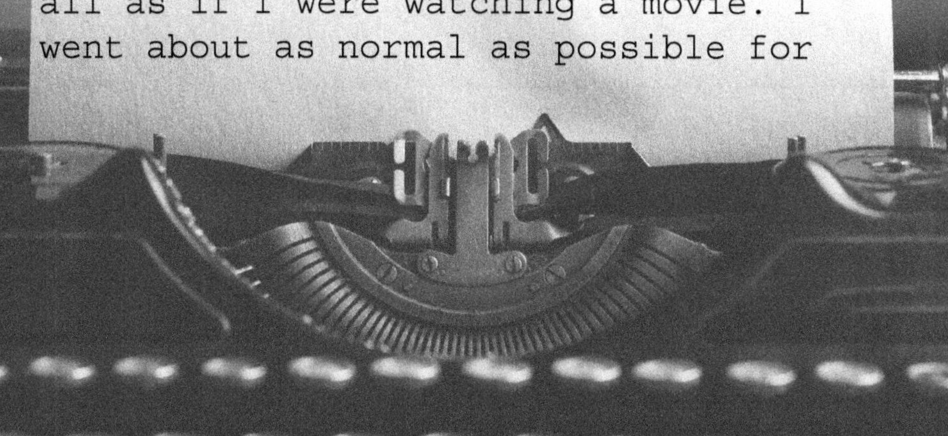

the next few days trying to pretend it wasn't there, but it kept resurfacing - to the point where it kept me up at night.

I just couldn't take it anymore. After several exhausting nights, I got out of bed and asked God, "Lord, what do you want me to do with this story?" And I promise you, on everything that I love, I heard a voice respond and say, "I want you to make this into a movie." Now, I've heard voices in my head before, both good and bad, but nothing like this. (Don't question it. Just roll with me here.) I immediately began to panic, not because I was hearing voices, but because I had no clue on how to make a movie.

Where do I even start?

The most logical place. Google. (Yes, Google was a thing in 2002.)
I began to research and from what I found, I concluded that I needed to write a script.

Here's some additional context to

help you visualize this story: I am
HORRIBLE at English and writing. (My
editor is on page six of this book and
I'm sure she is pulling her hair out
going through the first draft of this
book… lol.) Since I was a child, I
have always been able to TELL a really
good story. But when it came to the
functionality and structure of writing
in the English language, I just wasn't
good at it.

I remember having a tutor from 8th
grade through college to help with my
essays and papers. Since the 8th grade,
my tutors all had the same thing to say
when it came to my writing: the content
was good, but I wrote how I spoke.

I had no choice but to accept their
criticism and grew to be okay with it
until it didn't bother me at all.
But there I was, awake in the middle of

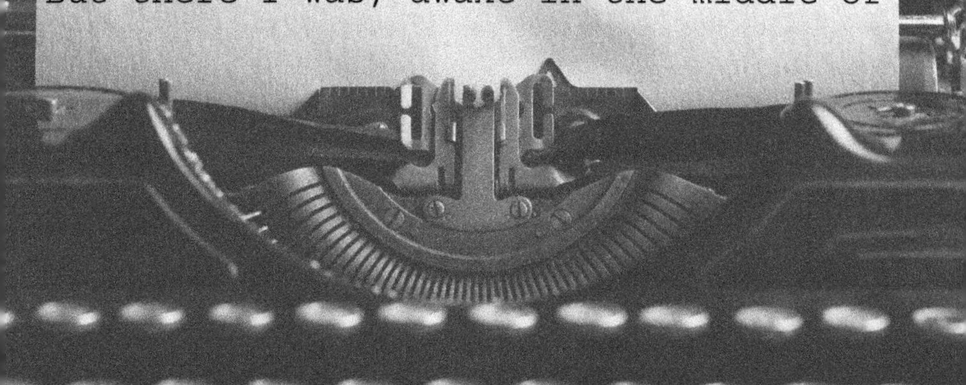

the night tasked to write a script from a story I had never seen nor heard in the material world - only in my head. For a minute I wanted to give up because I did not have a support system nor did I know anyone I could call to enlist help. Not one single person in my circle understood what I was talking about, let alone, had the slightest idea of where I should begin. My wife thought I was going crazy, and rightfully so. My friends didn't get it either, but the story would not go away! Completely discouraged, I was left to my own devices and had to simply figure it out.

After a few more days of googling, I finally found a script to read. Remember, this is 2002, and there is no centralized place to find film scripts as a regular person just googling "full movie scripts." So trust me when I say, I searched high and low to find what little I did.

I don't remember which movie script it was that I found, but I found one, and I was mortified! I did not understand it at all and it wasn't written like anything I had seen before.

There were words on the left side of the page.

There were words on the right side of the page.

There were some words dead smack in the middle.

It was as if I was reading a Japanese love story. It was written in English, but it was definitely in an entirely different language!

Now, I was super depressed because this story that was now inside of me was **NOT** going to be told because I had no idea how I was supposed to tell it through writing.

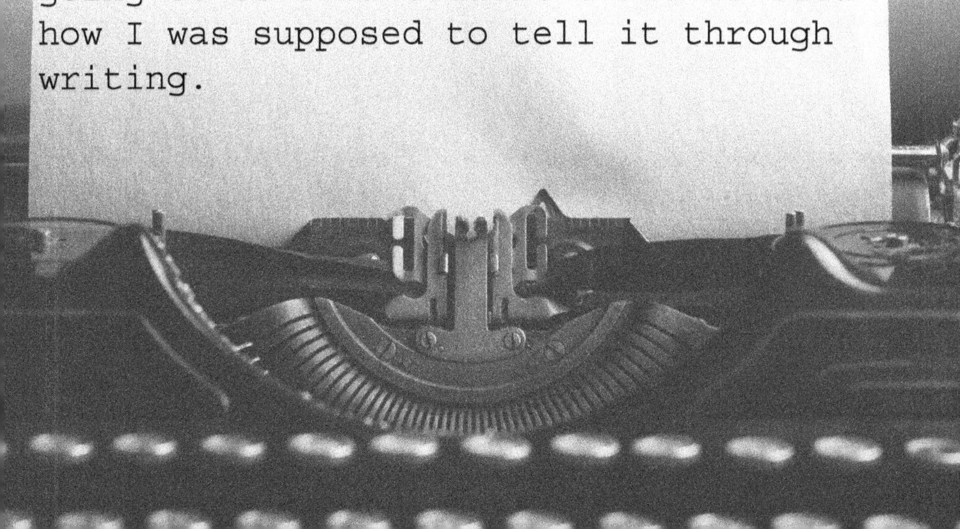

Then, one day thereafter, I heard the same Voice that told me to write the movie ask me, "What's your favorite movie?" Immediately, the film **INCEPTION** came to mind. From there, I just had to not only download the script for **INCEPTION**, but also watch the movie as I followed along with the script. The Voice let me know that this would be how I learned to write a script.

If you don't know me that well, then let me tell you that I am absolutely obsessed with **INCEPTION**. **INCEPTION** is, by far, my favorite movie, so I literally know it almost word for word. Motivated, I did another internet search. This time for **INCEPTION**. Once I found it, I hit the download button full of anxiety and excitement, pulled out my DVD copy of the movie, and headed straight over to my DVD player. and I found the script for **INCEPTION** and I downloaded it. Yes, I said, "my DVD and DVD player…" It's 2002, remember?

I hit play and started reading the script as I simultaneously watched

the action unfold on the television
screen. After the movie ended and I
reached the last page of the thick, one
hundred and twenty seven page packet I
printed out that was the script, I got
discouraged. After all of that, I still
didn't quite understand the language of
scriptwriting.

Instead of giving into my
disappointment, I decided to watch
INCEPTION yet again, but this time,
I would use my remote control to my
advantage. I read along with the
movie - the same as last time - but
I for sure wore out the pause button
my second, third, and millionth time
through.

Stopping at certain parts of the film
and reading the words on the page,
processing what I was watching on the
television and reading on the page,

I gradually began to understand this foreign language that is scriptwriting. I then started to study it, breaking the movie down minute by minute. I started noticing the timing of when specific elements and characters were introduced - in beats, in minutes, in scenes, in the actual storyline. Doing this, I noticed a pattern in the script that I had never noticed while watching the movie for the 100th time. I was amazed, to say the least, and this excited me.

From this point, I ran with this process and started my research on another movie - **PRINCESS BRIDE.** (Side note: if you've never watched **PRINCESS BRIDE**, find a way to watch it. It is a master class in the Art of storytelling.) Same as with **INCEPTION**, I watched **PRINCESS BRIDE** beginning to end with the script front and center. The more I read the script and watched the movie, the more I began to understand scriptwriting.

INCEPTION and PRINCESS BRIDE were very

similar in style. The heroes, the villains, and the conflict were each introduced on specific pages that drove the plot forward. This pattern showed me that screenwriting was nothing but repetition with different names and different characters.

All in all, I came to realize there was actually a formula for a good script! All I needed to do was fit my story inside of this formula and voila! I knew I would have a good script. Once this realization set in, I began my journey of writing my first script for the thriller/drama/suspense feature that had been keeping me awake for the past week.

LISTEN TO THE ANGELS came to be a story about the Fisk Jubilee Singers. Now, don't go running to Google trying to find this movie. It still has not been

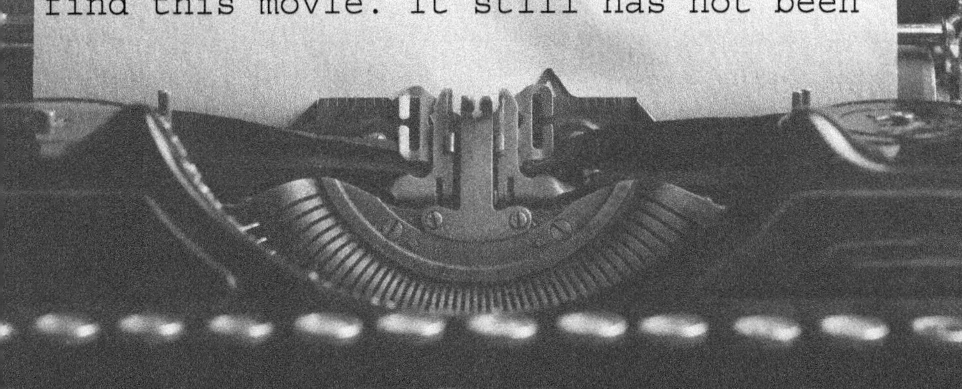

produced so let me save you some time. This movie played a major role in my life when it came to scriptwriting. 31 days further into 2002, I had finished 104 pages of this movie. It was official, my first script was complete.

Then, something strange happened.

Suddenly, five more stories dropped into my head and I knew I had to write their respective scripts. So, I got to writing. The next thing I knew, I had four completed first drafts. All done within 90 days.

YOU: SO, HOWARD, HOW DO I WRITE A SCRIPT?

Me: Think of your favorite movie, find the associated script online, and watch the movie while reading the script.

YOU: BUT HOWARD, MY FAVORITE MOVIE IS NOT IN THE SAME GENRE AS THE SCRIPT I WANT TO WRITE.

Me: To that I will say this: find a

successful movie in your specified
genre, find the associated script
online, and watch the movie while you
read the script.

It really is this simple.

Since my first attempt at
screenwriting, I have written a total
of forty-five scripts in different
genres for television and film. I've
won awards for my scripts, I've sold
quite a few of my scripts to other
filmmakers and television producers,
and I've produced movies and television
shows that came to life from my
scripts.

*YOU: HOWARD. WHY IS THE SCRIPT SO
IMPORTANT? I KNOW THE STORY I WANT TO
TELL. WHY CAN'T I JUST TELL IT?*

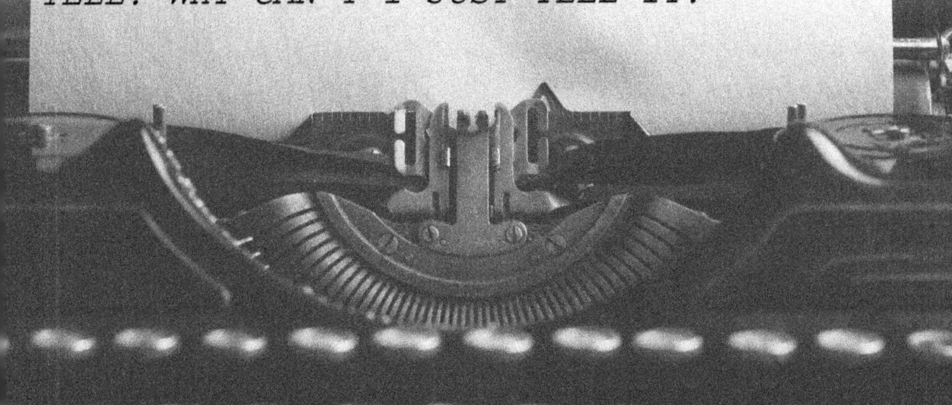

Me: Let's go back to the beginning of the story when I said that I looked at the script and it looked like a Japanese love letter to me. When you send your story to a producer or to a network or to anyone in the industry, that is exactly how they view your story if it's not formatted correctly. The story is essentially in a language that they cannot understand.

When these industry professionals are reading a script, they're also thinking about one hundred other things that are needed in order for that story to come alive and be made into a movie - the final product. So, when you tell them a story or just send over a story pitch or idea and there is no script included, it really handicaps them. This can be discouraging and they may, in turn, change their minds and no longer be interested in what you are pitching.

YOU: HOWARD, THEY HAVEN'T ASKED FOR A SCRIPT; THEY JUST WANT TO HEAR THE STORY.

Me: Make sure you read my other book in this series, HOW TO SELL YOUR TV SHOW/ MOVIE IN 31 DAYS. Sure, they like the story you pitched. Great. But trust me, they will ask you for the script after expressing interest. Now, do you really want to be in this huge meeting with people who are excited about your idea and you don't have all of the other elements they need in order to make a decision?
No, you don't.

Going back to **LISTEN TO THE ANGELS…** (Remember? The first script I ever wrote?) After I finished it, along with the others I mentioned, I edited them after learning more about screenwriting. From there, I thought it was a great idea to enter them into contests. Specifically, **LISTEN TO THE ANGELS** didn't win any contests, yet the other scripts did. This was a little confusing to me because why were the other stories from my small portfolio receiving great feedback, but this one was not? Regardless, I was just happy I had won. I wasn't complaining at all. But, 15 years later, I received a call from an agent in Hollywood. Yes, Hollywood. Los Angeles, California, Hollywood.

He got me on the phone and told me that he had just finished my script (**LISTEN TO THE ANGELS**) and wanted to offer me a contract for representation. I was confused because he didn't specify which script. I had entered all of them into competitions. He went on to tell me that this particular script didn't win any awards, but it was an honorable mention in one of the screenwriting competitions a few years ago.
"I love finding hidden gems in these contests," the agent told me. He praised me and indicated that he was perplexed because **LISTEN TO THE ANGELS** was "amazing, so he didn't understand why I hadn't been signed to an agency yet.

Saying I was surprised was an understatement. I never said **LISTEN TO THE ANGELS** was my "strongest" script. I never said it was my "best" script; it was simply my **FIRST** script. And to my shock, the first script that I ever wrote was the script that got me signed to a Hollywood agent, jump starting my filmmaking career.

I say all of that to say this… IT'S TIME TO WRITE YOUR FIRST SCRIPT!

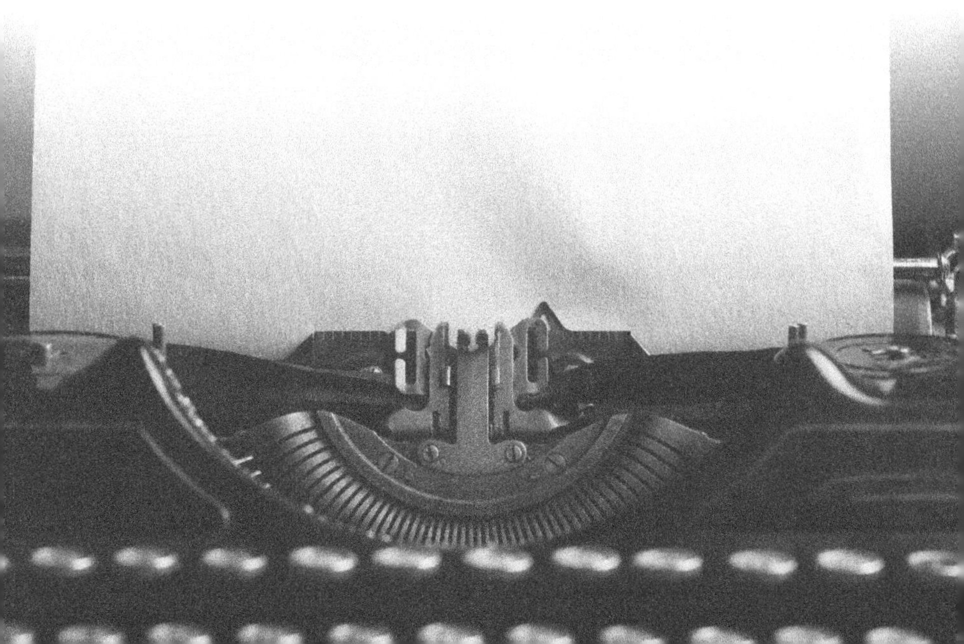

CHAPTER 2
WHERE DO I START?

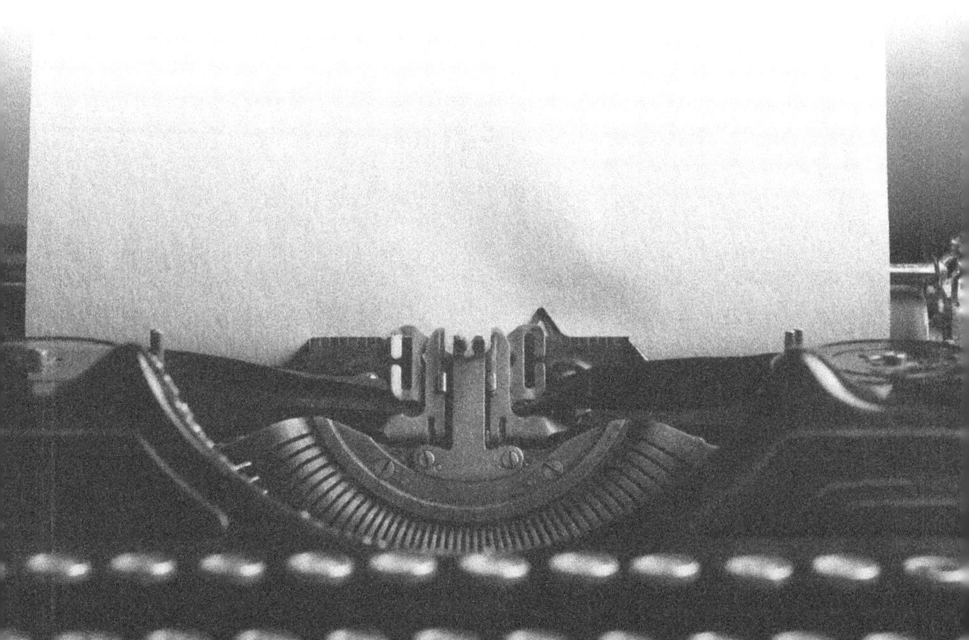

Now that we've discussed how you can learn to write a script, hopefully you've done that. Hopefully you found the script to your favorite movie/ TV show (or a movie in the same genre as your story) and practiced following along while watching the film.

It was fun, wasn't it?

Yeah, I was pretty excited when I did it the first time, too, and actually seeing the movie on paper was very breathtaking. Now, it's time for you to do the same with your story.

You: Howard, where do I start?
Me: You start from the beginning.

When it comes to writing a script for an original idea, don't complicate things.

Every story has a beginning, a middle, and an end. Your job is to piece those parts together and make it interesting for the reader - and ultimately, the viewer. So, when I say to just start

at the beginning, I mean simply that:
start at the beginning. Establish
the story, establish the hero, and
establish the world.

*You: Howard, what do you mean by
"world"?*

By "world" I mean the universe that the
story is written in. No. This does not
have to be some far off fantasyland. A
"world" exists whether the setting is a
western comedy or a horror drama.
We need to know where we are,
literally, so we need the universe and
the world of your story explained for
context. This is where you begin. Start
the story by placing the reader/viewer
in the world/universe and go from
there.

What time period does the story occur?

Where does the story happen?

Who does the story involve?

What is the psychological experience of the story?

How does the story unfold?

Who, what, when, where, how.

Basic storytelling mechanics.

The great thing about scriptwriting is that you can always go back and fill in parts you may have missed and you can always stop and start over as many times as you need. There is absolutely nothing wrong with that.

But what I really think people mean when they ask where they should begin with writing their script, is if they can actually start.

Remember I told you I was married and working full-time and that I was leading a choir, and I enjoyed it all? Well, I included this info so you could gather that I had very limited free time, if any. My life was quite complete and going very well. So, there was no real space for me to simply just sit down and focus to write a script. I was busy and responsible for a lot in my day-to-day life.

There are several factors that can prevent a person from starting and completing their script. Normally, these things may be considered after the script is complete, but I believe it is very important to lay this out on the table so you can figure out what you may need in order to make this script come to fruition. No need to avoid the obvious. So, let's address the elephant in the room...

8 FACTORS THAT CAN HOLD YOU BACK FROM BEGINNING OR COMPLETING YOUR SCRIPT

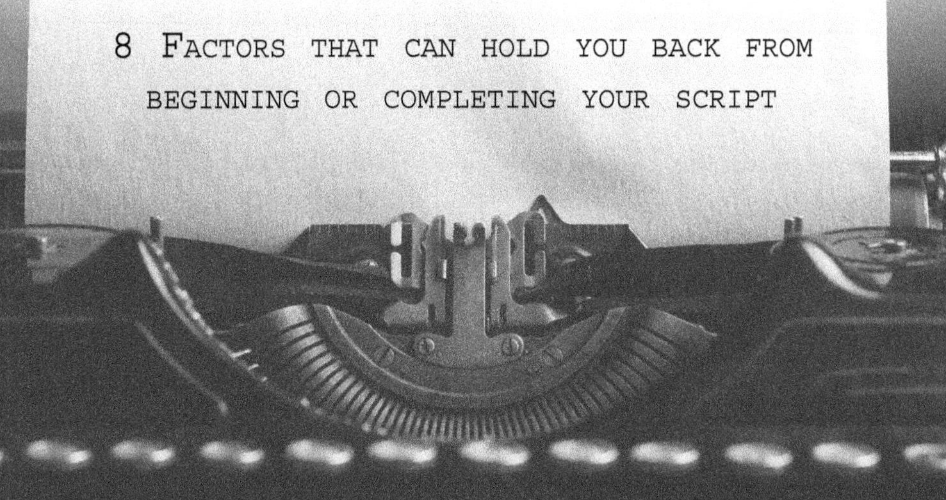

1. <u>Perfectionism</u>: Many writers struggle with perfectionism; feeling that their work is never good enough. This can lead to constant and continuous revisions and an inability to declare a script "finished." Stop comparing yourself to other writers and other creators. They have nothing to do with your journey. Your voice is your voice and no amount of perfectionism can take that away - nor even add to it. So, let's just throw perfectionism out the window.

2. <u>Self-doubt</u>: Writers may experience doubt about their abilities or the worthiness of their ideas leading to a lack of confidence in completing their script. Self-doubt may be a part of our everyday lives. For me, there isn't a day that goes by where I don't question if I am capable or have the capacity to do something - writing or otherwise. When it comes to my stories, I ask myself (and sometimes others, like my brother) if a script will ever get written or if people will enjoy what I've created. But, despite my concerns, none of this matters. At this point,

the only thing that matters is the
script.

3. <u>Lack of discipline</u>: Writing a
script requires consistent effort and
discipline if you are doing more than
just dabbling in it. Some individuals
may struggle to maintain a regular
writing schedule or prioritize their
creative work. If you know you don't
like discipline I need you to admit it
to yourself right now. You are going
to have to learn how to discipline
yourself in ways that will actually
work for you in order to complete this
script. No if, ands, or buts about it.
Find a time management or deep work
focusing technique you like and try it.
If it works, stick to it.

4. <u>Fear of failure</u>: The fear of
rejection or failure can be a
significant barrier to beginning and

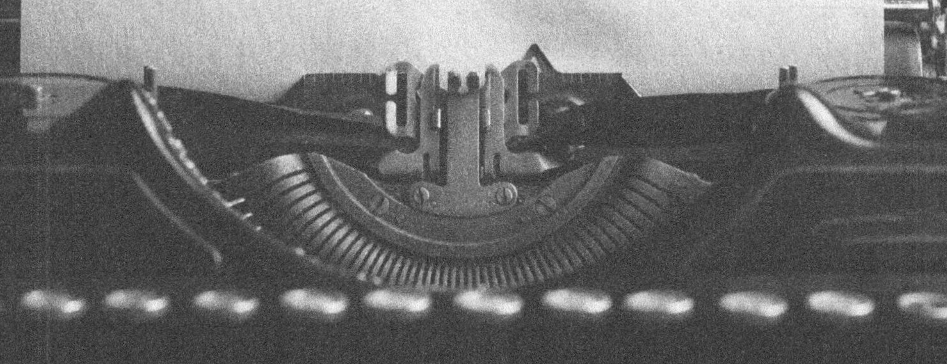

completing a script. Some writers may be hesitant to finish their work out of fear that it won't be well-received or that it won't meet their own expectations. Just a reminder, my first script **LISTEN TO THE ANGELS**, never won an award, was never bought, nor was it ever sold. Again, it wasn't my best work, but somehow it was the one that got me signed to an agency. Please keep this in mind when your fear of failure has you stalled with writing your script. Failure is a part of the story and it's a part of your story. So, do not be afraid of it. Embrace it, learn from it, and move forward, intentionally.

5. <u>Overwhelm</u>: Writing a script is a complex task that involves plotting, character development, dialogue, and more. Some writers may feel overwhelmed by the scope of the project, especially if they don't have a clear plan or outline. Hopefully, after reading this book, writing becomes less complex and makes more sense to you. Hopefully, after reading this, you will better understand plotting, character

development, and dialogue, amongst
other elements, so you can begin
your screenwriting journey in a more
confident and less chaotic manner.

6. _Distractions_: External distractions,
such as work, family responsibilities,
or personal commitments, can make it
difficult for writers to find the time
and focus needed to complete their
script. Let me stop you right here.
Distractions will never go away. So be
prepared to incorporate distractions
into your writing strategy. This
includes having solutions for the
distractions so you can finish your
script.

7. Lack of feedback or support: Without
encouragement, constructive feedback,
or a supportive community, writers may
feel isolated and unmotivated, which
can impede their progress. Now, the

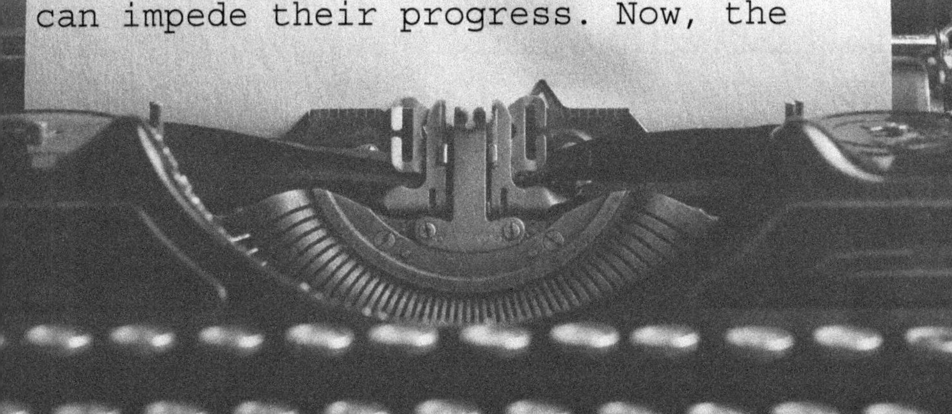

good thing about this point is that
over time, I've seen a significant
increase in supportive communities,
such as writing groups and filmmaking
networks and meetups all over social
media and event sites that can support
you in your screenwriting adventure.
But remember, everyone's journey is
different. Your journey will not
look like theirs. However, you will
have similar struggles and you'll be
equipped to help support each other and
hopefully, get you to the promised land
of having a completed script in hand.

8. <u>Unclear goals</u>: Some writers may
struggle to finish their script if they
lack a clear vision of what they hope
to achieve with their work, whether
it's seeking publication, production,
or personal satisfaction.
You only have one goal. Your one goal
is to write your script from start
to finish. You have limited control
over what happens after that point.
Generally, if you are not producing
the script yourself with your own film
crew and cast, you have no control on
whether your script is going to become

a television show, a three-part series, or a feature movie. From this moment, don't worry about the things you can't control. Focus on accomplishing the things you have full power over: starting and finishing your script.

Overcoming these barriers often involve addressing underlying fears, increasing self-awareness, developing effective writing habits, seeking adequate support, and finding strategies to manage time and distractions. Setting realistic goals, breaking the writing process down into manageable steps, and celebrating small achievements can help writers stay motivated and focused.
To recap, when you ask where you should start, I say start at the beginning…
of your doubt. You must know - without a shadow of a doubt, without anyone cheering you on, and without any guarantee - that this is going to work;

that this script is what you should be writing.

That's where it starts.

Your idea has to be so ingrained in your mind and your belief that your story has to be told - and told by you - has to be so strong in your heart in order to develop the motivation and inspiration you will need to complete your script. So, find your "why" and start at the beginning.

CHAPTER 3

TELEVISION OR FILM?

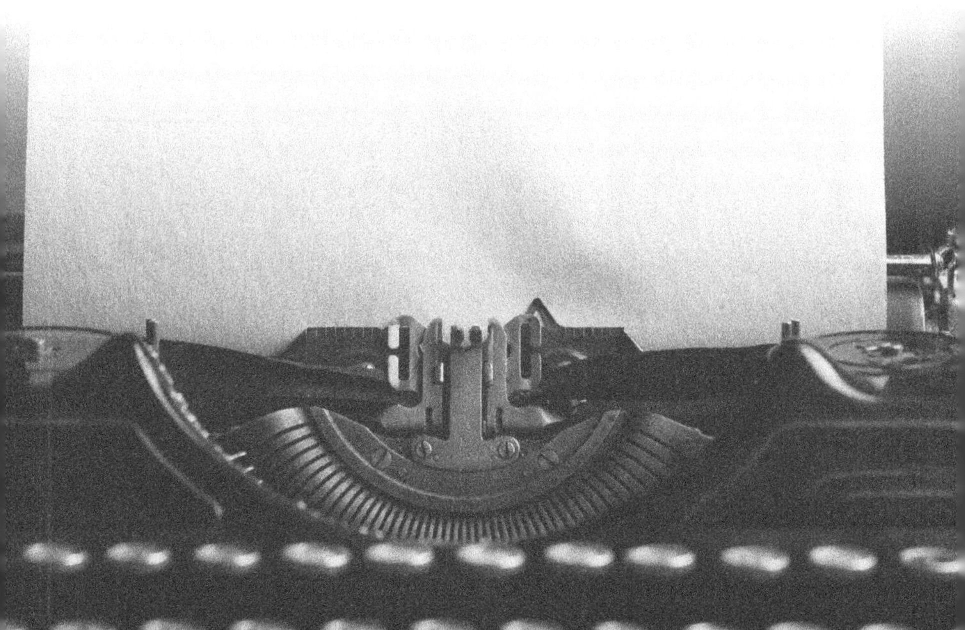

***Is there a difference between writing
for television and writing for film and
how do I tell which option is best for
my story?***

 Now, this is a loaded question.
It would probably take me two full
dedicated books to explain in detail.
But for the sake of this quick start
guide, I'll stick to the basics.
Firstly, I am not a specialist in
either, but I am going to provide you
with my opinion and some context by
telling you my journey.

When it comes to television writing
versus movie writing the differences
are major. With that said, know this:
it is much easier to convert a film
script into a television script once it
is done. Moving from television into
film can be a more challenging process.
This is because the movie script has
a beginning, middle, and ending. On
the other hand, scripts for television
series can go on for years and years
and never come to a full stop. Series
can potentially have an unlimited

number of seasons without the storyline
ever ending.

For an example, think about the last
time you may have read a novel cover
to cover, beginning to end. There were
points in the book where you may have
said to yourself, "this is a good place
to stop for tonight," and you place
your physical or digital bookmark in
that spot so you can return to start
up again the next time you pick up
the book to continue. This is what
happens at the end of each season of a
television show (unless the show ends
due to cancellation by the network or
it is literally the end of the story).

If you can complete a 90 plus-page
movie script, whoever may be interested
in it - producer, network, or
production company, they will be able
to decide if it would be best for a

made for TV movie, a three-part series, or something else.

This is out of your control at this point, so don't worry yourself about this process right now. The only thing you need to concern yourself with is writing a great story and formatting an amazing script.

Again, this is all just my opinion so someone else can tell you something different and I will completely understand if it works better for them or for you. To each their own. But I've written over fifteen scripts for television and over thirty film scripts. It is much harder for me to write a script for TV than it is for me to write a movie script for so many different reasons. But without getting caught up in the logistics and semantics of film versus TV, let's just focus on the script itself and why it's important to have it.

*THE TOP 10 REASONS WHY YOU
NEED A MOVIE SCRIPT*

1. <u>Storytelling:</u> A movie script is essential for telling a compelling story through film, with well-developed characters, plot, and dialogue.

2. <u>Planning:</u> Having a script helps in planning out the scenes, shots, and overall structure of the film before production begins. Even though production is further down the line, this is something very important to know when it comes to screenwriting.

3. <u>Communication:</u> A script serves as a blueprint for the entire film production team, ensuring everyone is on the same page regarding the vision for the movie. Think of the script being the backbone and foundation of the entire film. Without it, everything would fall apart.

4. <u>Budgeting:</u> A well-written script

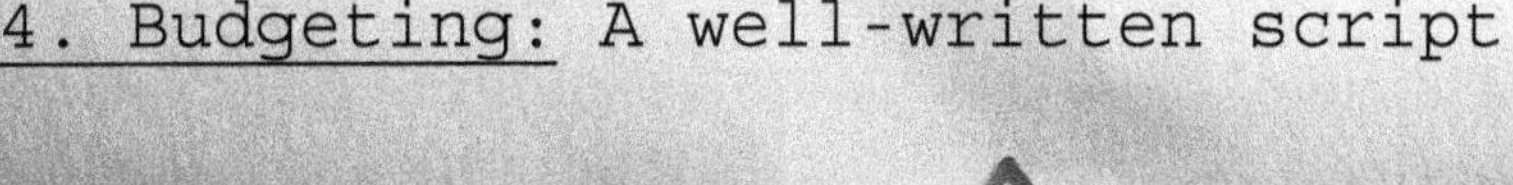

can help with estimating the budget needed for the entire film production by outlining the locations, props, and special effects required. We'll touch on budgeting later in this book once we get some more information about the script.

5. Casting: A script is crucial for casting actors, as it provides a clear idea of the characters and their arcs in the story.

6. Legal Protections: A script can help protect your ideas and intellectual property by establishing your ownership and rights to the story. This is extremely important. You cannot copyright an idea of words, but if you format it properly into a script - whether screenplay or stage play, then that can be copyrighted. Think of it this way: you can copyright a script, you can't necessarily copyright the note on your iPhone about your screenplay idea from last year.

7. Editing: A script provides a framework for editing and refining the

story before and during production to ensure a cohesive final product.

8. Pitching: If you plan to pitch your movie idea to producers or studios, a script is essential to showcase your vision and storytelling abilities.

9. Collaboration: A script facilitates collaboration between writers, directors, producers, and other creatives involved in the filmmaking process.

10. Production: Ultimately, a script is the foundation of any successful movie production, guiding the entire filmmaking process from pre-production to post-production. I know you probably heard this saying: "show me a bad movie and I'll show you a bad script." There is no way to fix a bad movie but there is a way to fix a bad script.

These reasons all highlight the importance of a well-crafted movie script in bringing a film to life and ensuring its success.

I said all of that to say that I don't want you to focus on whether it's a TV story or a film or whatever. I want you to focus on getting the story on paper and properly telling the beginning, middle, and end. That's all.
...For now.

CHAPTER 4
AFTER I FINISH THIS SCRIPT, HOW MUCH WILL I MAKE FROM IT?

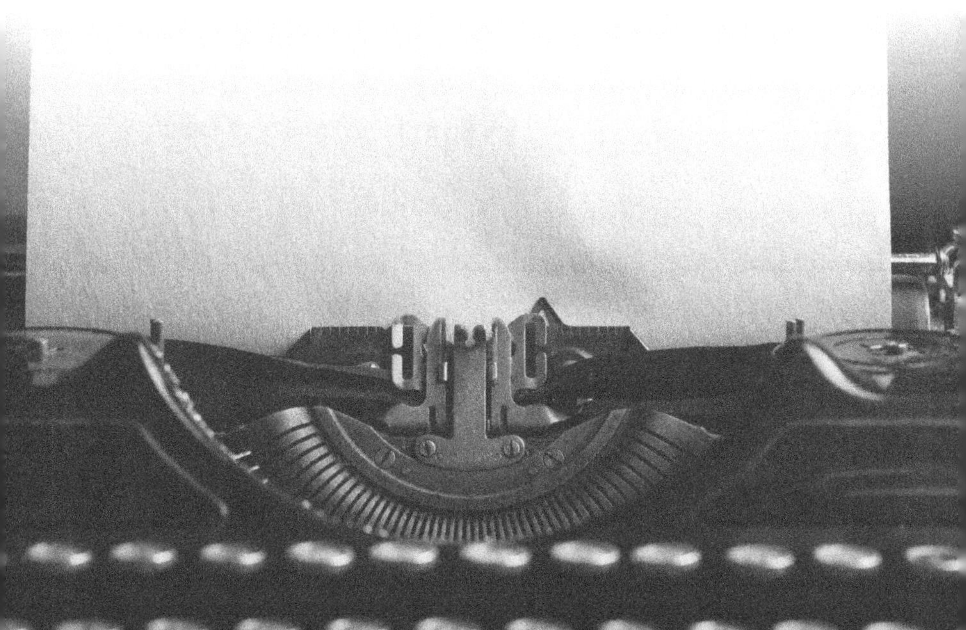

SHOW ME THE MONEY!

Plenty of people get upset about this question, but not I. I actually think it is a very legitimate question.

Along my journey, I've found there exist two different types of screenwriters. One who writes for the love of creating and another who writes for money. Neither one of them is wrong in their pursuit and neither one is supposedly right.

As always, remember that this is your journey - no one else's - so if someone is writing for money and to make a career of screenwriting, then congratulations to them! If someone is writing for a hobby, their church, their school project, or just for fun, again, congratulations. Let's not judge one side more than the other because screenwriting is an Art. Once you finish writing a script, you are effectively an artist and that script is your masterpiece. Whether you're looking to sell it and move on or whether you're looking to put it on the shelf and admire it, both are the same and both should be commended because only 1% of 1% of people in the world are screenwriters. Their "whys" don't and shouldn't matter to you.

Now, back to the question. How much could you expect to make from your script? Honestly, I don't know. When brand new filmmakers ask me this question, I interpret it to mean that they are looking to get rich from this story or from screenwriting, in general. It's quite possible to make a lot of money from writing and it's very possible to make little to no money.

I promise I'm not trying to avoid the question nor am I making light of the inquiry, but really, there is no clear answer because everyone's journey is different. If you're looking to make this your career, I'm going to tell you

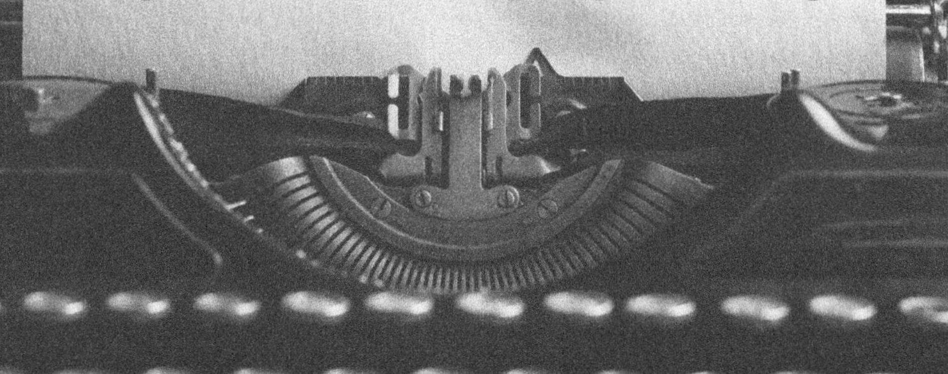

what a studio producer told me just a few years ago. When you write, write a story that the world needs to see but that can only be told by you.
Let me say that again.

You want to write something that the world needs to see but can only be told by you.

Additionally, career-minded folks should consider writing smaller budget films in addition to big budget movies. This is because smaller budget films (think made for TV movies or "Tubi-esque" type of films) are easier to sell in my opinion and could potentially bring you a steadier stream of income versus you fighting tooth and nail trying to sell "the one."

And if "numbers" is your thing, simply download the **"WGA Schedule of Minimums."** In that download you will find the prices that WGA requires for union based films.

In the next chapter, I will go more into detail about how to write your script for different genres, but overall, try to keep in mind the potential budget of the movie when writing your script. Now, that's not to say that high budget films don't get produced. I have a colleague I know personally who wrote and sold just one big budget script. Congratulations are in order for him, but I caution you because this is not the norm.

Lastly, if you are looking to make screenwriting your career, be prepared to write other people's stories. Yes, ghostwriting and co-writing is a significant way to make money. This path can help you hone your skills, build a network, and learn even more about the industry depending on your clientele and specialities. This can be a huge money maker for you unless your potential future clients all decide to purchase this book as well and learn

how to write for themselves... But I
digress.

Let me introduce you to **_MILE 19_**. My
baby. **_MILE 19_** is the first feature
film I wrote and produced and directed.
After I signed on with my agent, I
moved out to Los Angeles, California
- to Hollywood. It was thee absolute
greatest decision I've ever made. I was
essentially homeless for a brief period
of time when I touched down in the
city, but it was all very much worth
it.

Back to **_MILE 19_**...
Once I moved to LA, I was able to make
some great connections and build my
network with some great people in the
film industry. I ended up meeting and
working for a producer who worked on
Steven Spielberg projects. He wanted
me to join him on a current project he
was attempting to sell overseas because
he needed a writer. Once I had all
the information necessary, I started
developing his idea by formatting it
into a script and creating the synopsis
for the story.

<u>Did I mention I did it all for no pay?</u> Yeah. I did not get paid for my services. I opted to do this willingly. One day he called a meeting with me at a fancy restaurant in Beverly Hills and I just knew he was about to tell me that he's officially hiring me and will be paying me very well. I was so excited! If you know me, you know I don't get excited about much, so this had to be worth something. I just knew that this was about to be the biggest day of my life since I signed with my agent. My dream was unfolding in record time!

I went through my suitcases and found the best shirt and cleanest pants that made the trek across the country with me. Yes, I was living out of suitcases at this time. I put my clothes on, had the hugest grin on my face, and the tightest knots in my belly as I stared

at myself in the mirror ready to meet
with my destiny!

I drove to the fancy restaurant in
Beverly Hills with the anticipation of
becoming the next great screenwriter in
the world - or at least in Hollywood.
I drove around the restaurant several
times, noticing that there was only
paid parking available, including
valet, and I had no money. When I say,
"no money," I mean I had a total dollar
in my bank account and cup holder full
of pennies, that was less than what
parking cost.

I was so pumped up for this meeting,
I made sure to arrive early so that I
could be on time. I ended up parking
four blocks away from the restaurant
in an alley. I grabbed my bag and
walked to the restaurant. The walk
was about 30 minutes long. Of course
when I walked through the doors of
the building, I was met with some
judgemental looks, because my clothes
and apperance had changed a little from
that walk, but it didn't bother me. I
knew from the moment I saw there was

only paid parking outside that I was clearly out of my league , but I knew this would be where my life changed for the better.

The hostess sat me in the lobby as I waited on the producer to arrive. I waited and waited somemore. I was staring out the window like I was waiting for my dad after football practice. Finally, he arrived 2 hours after our agreed upon appointment time. I was still unfazed because this would be the meeting of all meetings. When he finally met up with me, I stood to greet him and I guess he noticed the excitement and anticipation in my eyes and his energy immediately seemed to shift.

The hostess seats us and we start going over the project right away. The conversation flowed and he told me his

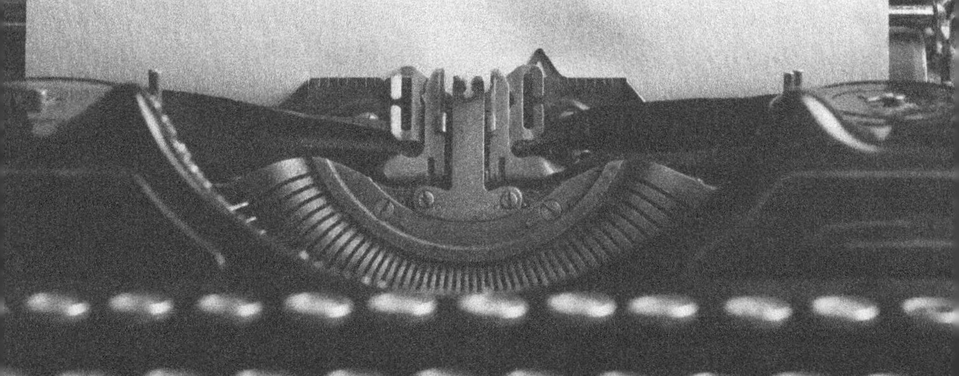

plans and what he needed from me within the specified timeframe. I was super giddy and excited because I was ready and anticipating the moment for me to say, "yes, I accept this job and you can pay me X amount of dollars."
That moment never came.

He spoke about his project and what he needed, closed his computer, and got ready to leave the restaurant. I was devastated, confused, and heartbroken. I didn't quite know what went wrong. Everything was on track; the stars were (supposed to be) aligning. This man had been working with me for over a month at this point, so he knew I was talented. He knew I was professional. He knew I could get the job done. What happened?

I couldn't take it anymore and as he was packing his stuff, I blatantly said, "so, you're not interested in hiring me." He stood there for a beat and looked at me.

Seemingly confused, he tilted his head and asked, "Oh! You thought I was going

to offer you a job?" I discouragingly
nodded my head, yes. He looked at me,
sat back down in his chair, and he told
me that he was unable to hire me at
that time because he didn't have the
budget for the project as of yet. But
instead offered me "some great advice"
that would be helpful for my future.
Defeated, I didn't want to leave the
restaurant and this meeting empty-
handed. I sat back down across from
him in this fancy Beverly Hills
establishment where I clearly did
not fit, and listened to his advice.
Afterall, he was a 20-year vet in the
film industry.

I pushed down the painful realization
that I had literally been working for
free for the last month and a half.
I swallowed the fact that we had no
paperwork nor contracts nor any other
evidence that I had done any of the

work I submitted to him. I was torn apart internally because I would not receive any credit for my hefty contribution. …but, I believed that his advice would be worth it.

After a moment, he says, "Howard, you are a very, very talented writer and you will be very successful in this industry, but honestly, it's going to take you about six years to get into a writing room or to sell something."

My heart dropped.

My emotions were already all over the place, so to hear what he had to say was like getting shot from the front and the back at the same time. "Let me tell you how you can turn those 6 years into 3 years." He continued, "write a script or find one of your old scripts and get it made into a movie. Once it is in movie form, people will recognize your greatness." He stood up again, finished packing his belongings, shook my hand, and walked out of the room.

That was it.

I sat there for about another thirty minutes going through a series of emotions. Honestly, I didn't know how to feel. On one hand, he just complimented me and told me to my face that I was a great writer and I would make it in this industry. Yet, on the other hand, he also just told me that he couldn't hire me for a project I was actively working on - for free - for whatever reason. He saw my value, but couldn't pay my worth. He saw my skill, but couldn't officially hire me. He saw my potential, but couldn't see how it could fit into his professional life.

I finally mustered up enough strength to get up from my chair, walk towards the door, and say goodbye to the hostess. She could see the disappointment in my eyes. In true hospitality fashion, she inquired about the meeting, asking me if it went well. I looked back at her and told her I thought so with a defeated, yet appreciative smile.

After a few months passed, I completed the work the producer and I agreed upon and I sent it over. Needless to say, I didn't hear from him again. What he said stuck with me. He gave me this advice for a reason. What could I take from it? He could have very easily said, "good luck, kid," and sent me on my way. But he didn't. He could have told me to go back to Georgia and that I would make a great manager. He could have told me the industry was saturated and that I should quit. He could have told me anything that could have influenced me in a lot of different ways, but he didn't and I couldn't forget what he said.

He told me that I would be great in this industry and I believed him. So, I did what he told me to do. I found a script I wrote a while back, edited it to certain specifications, and I took every penny that I had (and a few other people's pennies) and produced

MILE 19. Exactly three years after that meeting, I began my professional career in Hollywood.

Yes, studying screenwriting was one thing. But the business of screenwriting was another. I sold the ***MILE 19*** script to myself for $1. Despite this miniscule sale of my script, I could tell you that from that moment on, I have been rich. Of course, it wasn't about the amount of the money for the script, but rather, it was the experience.

My experience up until that point taught me such priceless lessons that could never be taught in a classroom nor any other formal setting. …and trust me, you definitely can't learn it from someone simply telling you about it; you have to experience it. Since the production of ***MILE 19*** in 2020 -

yes, during the global pandemic, I've sold many scripts and I have been hired to write as many scripts as I have sold. I believe this has been possible due to my trial by fire.

You may want to ask which category of screenwriter I fall into. Am I a hobbyist or am I a career writer? Well, I'll tell you. After I finished my first script, I knew I wanted to make a career out of this, so I wrote stories I felt would sell. I specialize in writing scripts in the $1M to $5M range. I also have a quick turnaround in order to meet the needs of indie producers. I was able to transform their expensive scripts into budget-friendly ones so they would be able to produce their projects themselves. Independent filmmakers are a huge market. So, I marketed myself to those I felt needed my services and I knew I would be able to expand from there.

So, to answer your question about income and how much you could make from your script, I still dont have a number for you. But what I do know is that you will be rich once you go through this journey!

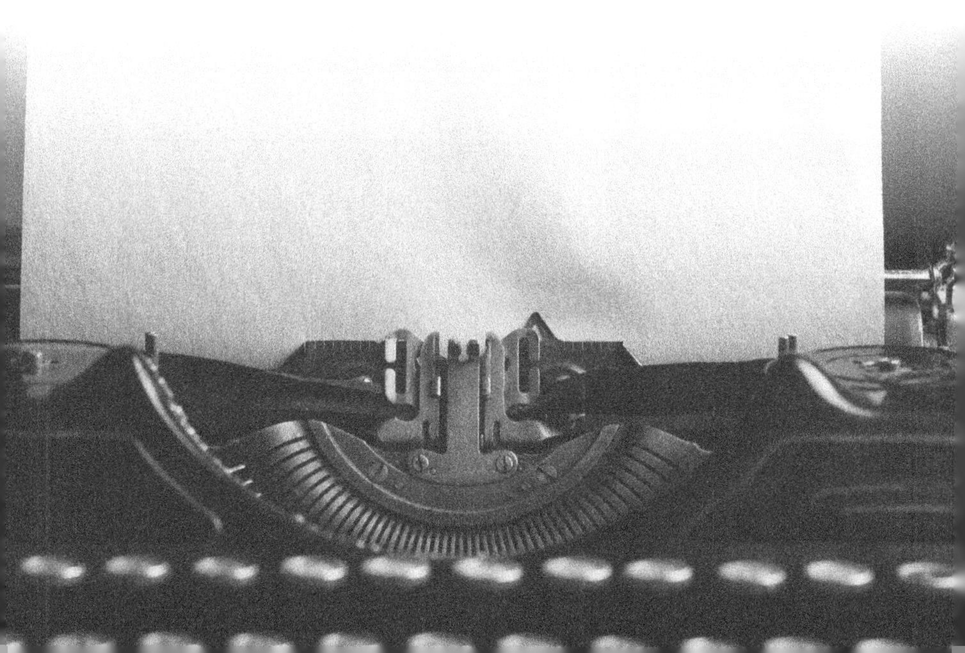

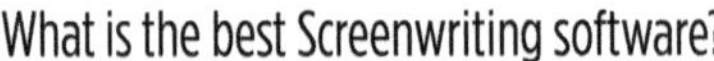
What is the best Screenwriting software?

CHAPTER 5

WHAT IS THE BEST SCREENWRITING SOFTWARE?

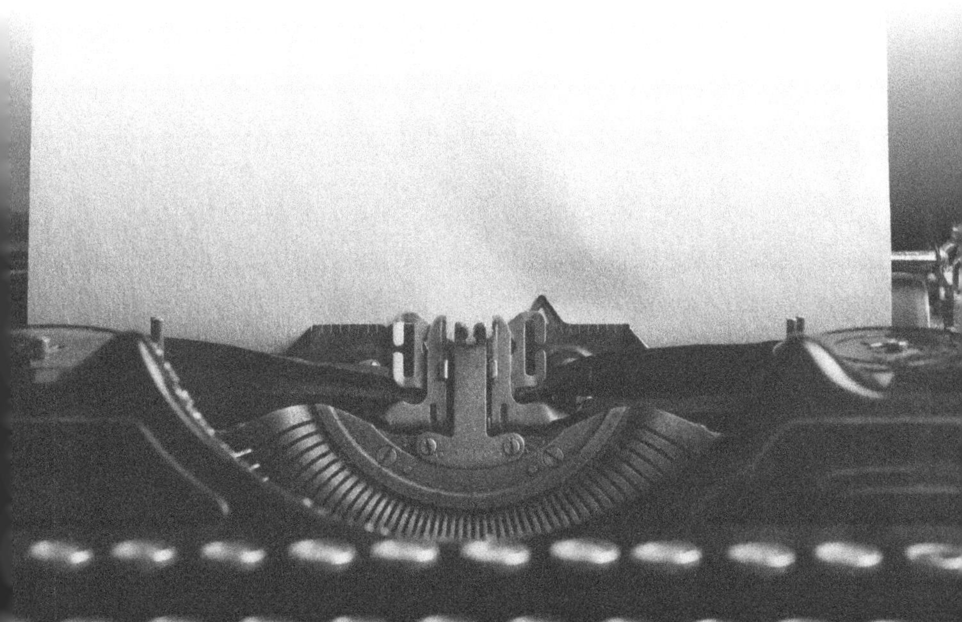

When it comes to technology, a lot has changed since 2002 and most of it has changed for the better. When I first started writing, I was broke. I didn't have any extra money for any type of document software, let alone scriptwriting software. The program I started writing with *(I think it was called, Scribe, or something like that. Honestly, I don't remember.)* doesn't even exist anymore. At the time, it was free and it was exactly what I needed to begin my journey.

After I wrote my first version of my first script, I ended up upgrading to a scriptwriting-specific program called, Final Draft. Since then, it's been what I have used to write my scripts.

Final Draft is the industry standard and it has so many features, including some default scripts for you to look over and practice your writing. It also includes tutorials, writing help, and the ability to collaborate with others at a distance in real time.

My suggestion would be to purchase either the desktop version or the app subscription of Final Draft. It will be extremely helpful to start out doing as much as you can by industry standards so you don't have to adjust later - which will save you a lot of time and frustration.

Compared to 2002, everything is a lot more inexpensive and there are some other great screenwriting programs on the market currently that you will find to be easy to work with, but my suggestion and go-to is Final Draft. I suggest using Final Draft because your files can be opened anywhere on any device with the program running. Also, I've heard some horror stories where whole scripts have been deleted, pages were out of order, and overall editing was atrocious all because of user error

trying to convert and send files not in
Final Draft (.fdx). Don't let this be
you.

I've learned my lesson through other
people's experience and I've avoided
this as much as possible. When
submitting my script for a competition,
to an agent, or to a production
company, I want it to be the best that
it can be. This includes the formatting
and file type.

Let me tell you something about
producers, directors, and production
companies. Most of the time they are
looking for reasons to not like your
script. So, any little thing that is
even a slight deviation from what they
normally see and interact with in their
day-to-day can be used as justification
for why your script was rejected.
This sentiment goes for contests and
competitions as well. You will hear
a lot of professionals say they know
whether or not they want to work on the
project by the first two to ten pages.
Because this is the case, you want to
make sure that the program you use to

write those first two to ten pages (and
ultimately, the entire script) is the
best program out there for you to use.
Sometimes you only get one shot, so
make it your best one.

If you're concerned about cost,
I say look at Final Draft as an
investment. You'll definitely get
your return on investment if you take
screenwriting seriously. However, I
totally understand sticker shock.
Final Draft offers lots of discounts,
including student pricing and seasonal
promotions. It's worth it to look into
what is available once you start the
free trial or do additional research.
Again, I suggest Final Draft because
of all their benefits, features, and
the fact that it is industry standard.
There are some other excellent programs
and software tools available to help
you write your script efficiently.

HERE ARE SOME POPULAR OPTIONS USED BY MANY SCREENWRITERS:

1. **Final Draft**: Final Draft is one of the most widely used screenwriting software programs in the industry. It offers features specifically designed for screenwriters, such as industry-standard formatting, collaboration tools, and script versioning.

2. **Celtx**: Celtx is a versatile scriptwriting software that allows you to write scripts, storyboard, and collaborate with team members. It is available both as a desktop application and an online platform.

3. **WriterDuet**: WriterDuet is a cloud-based screenwriting software that enables real-time collaboration with other writers. It is known for its user-friendly interface and robust features.

4. **Fade In**: Fade In is a professional screenwriting software that offers a clean interface,

industry-standard formatting, and compatibility with various file formats. It is popular among both aspiring and professional screenwriters.

5. **Scrivener**: While Scrivener is not specifically designed for screenwriting, it is a powerful tool for organizing and writing long-form projects, including scripts. It offers a range of features for structuring and outlining your script.

6. **Movie Magic Screenwriter**: Movie Magic Screenwriter is yet another popular choice for screenwriters, offering industry-standard formatting, collaboration tools, and the ability to import and export files in different formats.

These are just a few options available

for writing your script. The best program for you will depend on your personal preferences, budget, and specific needs as a writer. It may be helpful to explore trial versions or demos of these programs to find the one that works best for you.

CHAPTER 6
WHAT KIND OF SCRIPT SHOULD I WRITE FIRST?

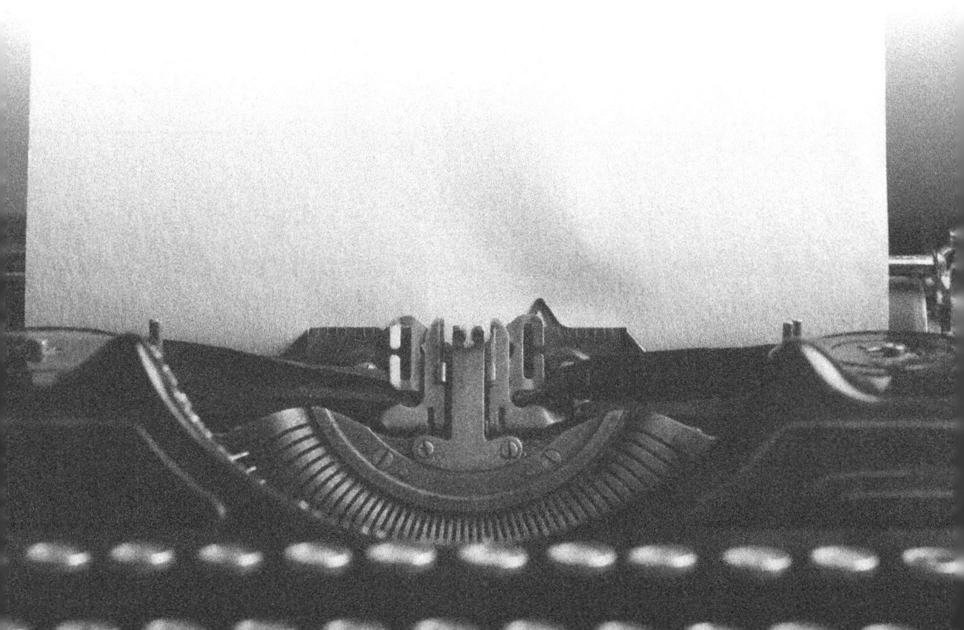

This is actually a very important question. What kind of script should I write first?

If you're anything like me, I'm going to assume that you have at least 60 ideas floating around that you want to make into scripts. More than likely, all 60 of your ideas are originals that you created in your mind or with the help of some other original story, or "IP" (intellectual property).

I believe the script you should write first is the one that you're the most passionate about. Passion plays a huge part in how you write, how you pitch, and how you work. (Remember, we talked about discipline?) The more passionate you are about the script, the faster you can finish it and you will probably create a really strong draft where you allow yourself to flow and be the most creative.

Passion can serve as a motivator when you "don't feel like it." Passion serves as a tool and can help you when

you're pitching your script and story
to others. Passion outweighs excuses
when you need that final push to finish
the project. So, before you decide on a
genre, before you decide on the number
of pages, before you decide on anything
else, make sure you have passion for
the project you are writing.

Next, conduct some market research.
Many people new to industry will
not have access to this privileged
information. This is simply because
generally only agents and aggregators
are privy to this info. But, if you
put your researching hat on, you'll
soon find out that there are a few
hints floating around that can help you
identify what studios, producers, and
networks are looking for.

Be sure to check IMDb (The Internet
Movie Database). It is essentially

a database of all movies, television shows, shorts, etc. and the casts and crews of the productions. It has production information, including pre- and post- production, along with a gambit of other relevant information. IMDb can let you know what movies and shows are slated to release. Google IMDb and begin your research.

Another major tool that helped me out in the beginning is a website called, InkTip.com. It is a site that provides info about what scripts producers are looking for currently. InkTip also has a job board of sorts for writers and filmmakers. Writers have gained notable representation, in addition to steady work from InkTip.com, so I highly recommend checking it out for yourself. The last thing I would consider when thinking about what type of script I should write is who is paying me for the job. If you will be writing a script from someone else's idea, then obviously, this will take precedence over you writing for yourself at this time if screenwriting is your career goal.

SIDE NOTE: When you're writing scripts for other people, stay inside of their world. Stay within the constraints of their story.
Tell their story, use their characters, describe their villains. Be sure to produce a strong script that will help move not only their career forward, but yours as well. This isn't your story. So don't drop your influences or your voice into their script. You may not agree with what the protagonist does or you may not agree with how the antagonist behaves, but it isn't your call. They hired you to write their script. It's okay to have suggestions or notes, but make sure your notes are within the confines of the universe they have already created. Trust me, there's nothing worse than a screenwriter who is overly opinionated about someone else's story that they

have been hired to write. It's annoying and can come off as unprofessional.

So, to answer the question, "what type of script should I write first?", consider market trends, audience preferences, and potential buyers.

HERE'S A LIST OF SOME SCRIPT TYPES THAT ARE OFTEN HIGHLY SOUGHT AFTER:

1. **High-concept scripts**: These scripts have a unique and compelling premise that can be easily pitched in a few words. They often combine familiar genres in innovative ways. Think of OCEANS 8 or the JAMES BOND universe.

2. **Genre scripts**: Scripts in popular genres such as action, thriller, comedy, sci-fi, and horror tend to have broader appeal and are more likely to attract buyers.

3. **Adaptations**: Scripts based on popular books, comics, or true stories have built-in audiences and can be attractive to producers looking for pre-existing material.

4. **Character-driven scripts**: Well-developed characters with depth and complexity can make a script stand out and appeal to actors looking for challenging roles. Consider superhero films and shows that revolve around a specific character and their life. President Lincoln comes to mind here.

5. **Diverse and inclusive scripts**: Stories that feature diverse characters and perspectives are increasingly in demand in the industry.

6. **TV pilot scripts**: With the rise of streaming platforms, there is a growing demand for original TV series concepts and pilot scripts.

7. **Low-budget scripts**: Scripts that can be produced on a modest budget are often attractive to independent

filmmakers and production companies. Networks like Tubi thrive on low-budget scripts.

8. **Scripts with a strong emotional core**: Stories that evoke strong emotions or explore universal themes can resonate with a wide audience.

Ultimately, the best script to write with the intention of selling is one that showcases your unique voice and storytelling abilities while also aligning with current market trends and industry demands. Remember to research the market, stay true to your vision, and be open to feedback and collaboration.

CHAPTER 7

WHAT DO THESE WORDS MEAN?

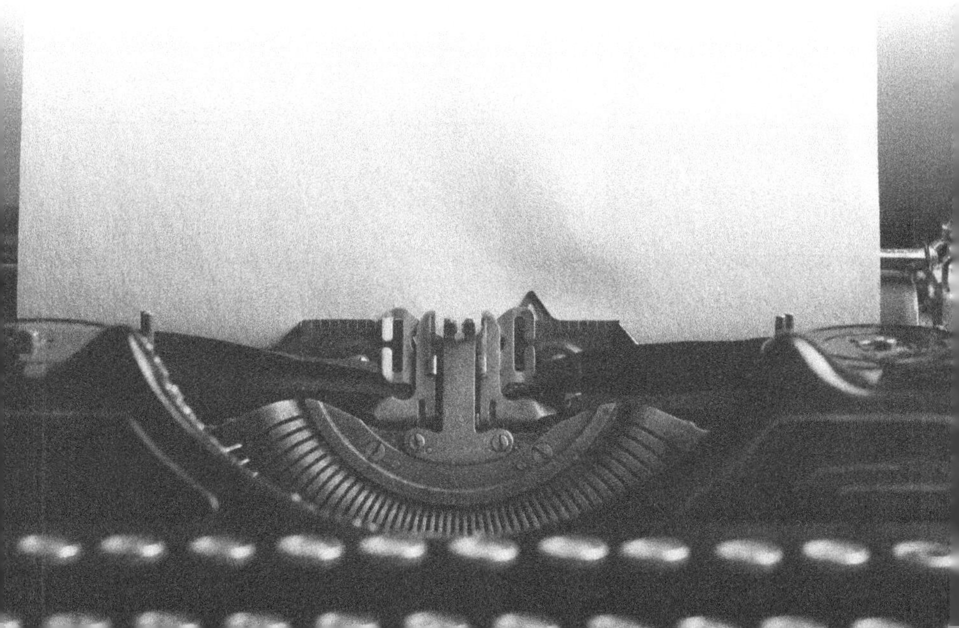

I know you are looking at the script that you download and are like, what do these words mean.

Remember the Japanese love letter I spoke about from Chapter 1? It was the only way I could describe how a script looked to me my first time seeing one… a foreign language I couldn't understand nor figure out how to translate. I now know that scriptwriting is a language in itself. For you to properly write scripts, you're going to have to learn the foundation of that language. There is no fancy story that goes behind this; it simply requires some work.

To be honest, everything we've talked about so far hasn't even started the clock on your 31 days of writing. Before you can even think about writing, you have to perform research to prepare and set yourself up for success. One of the best books I recommend when it comes to learning the language of scriptwriting in the most basic way is, **_Screenwriting for Dummies._** As an alternative, you can

just Google "screenwriting words"
or "screenwriting dictionaries" and
everything will be explained to you.
I didn't have this option in 2002,
but you have it now in addition to a
plethora of reading materials that
will allow you to become familiar with
the language being used in industry-
standard scripts.

Using industry-standard language
is very important because if your
intended audience (producers, networks,
affiliates, etc.) can't understand your
script, they can't see your vision and
they can't understand your story. If
they can't understand your story nor
see your vision, they aren't going to
be interested in it enough to buy it,
produce it, or option it. So, take the
time necessary to become familiar with
this new language. You don't have to
become an expert today; just become

familiar.

This language, along with proper
formatting, brings people into your
mind so they can better understand
the purpose of your story. Plenty of
scripts people have sent for me to
look over are missing some crucial key
elements. This alone takes me away from
the story. I cannot become engrossed
in their world because I am too busy
trying to figure it out for myself.
This is what causes me to end up
missing the point of the story.
Everything in your script should move
the story forward. Let me repeat:
Everything in your script should move
the story forward.

If something doesn't help the story,
cut it out of the script. As you're
learning the words and elements
specific to screenwriting, learn the
ones that will be the most important
to you and your script. For example, if
you have a script that doesn't involve
any voiceovers nor any off-camera
voices, then don't spend a lot of time
trying to figure out when to use these

elements. Focus on the ones that will actually help you write your story and make your script the best it will be. There are several ways to do things right, but there is only one way to get things wrong. Just to remind you, producers, directors, and production companies are doing their best to not approve your script, so you have to make sure the basics are presented properly. So, do the work, do the research, and do the preparation before you write your script.

In scripts, certain terms, including those related to the technical aspects of filmmaking, are crucial for conveying the story effectively to professionals.

HERE ARE 10 IMPORTANT TERMS COMMONLY USED IN SCRIPTS AND THE FILM INDUSTRY:

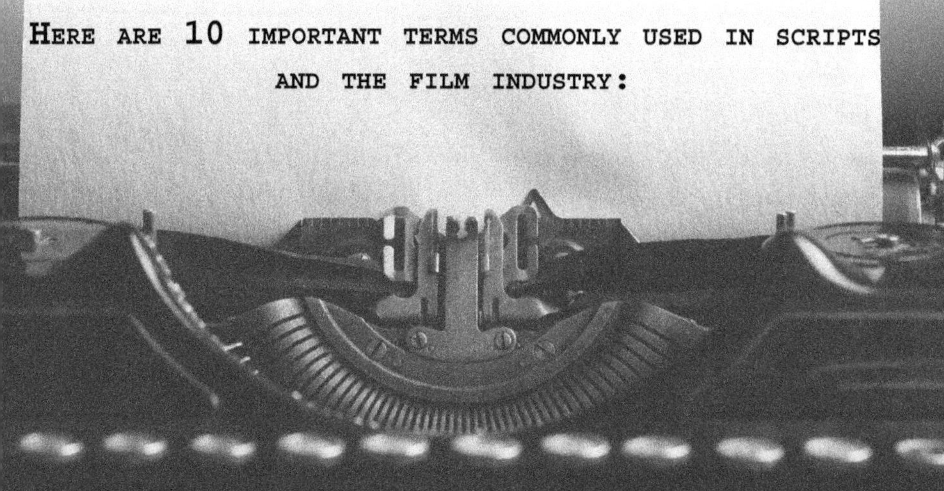

1. <u>Action</u>: Specifies what is happening in a scene.

2. <u>Dialogue</u>: The spoken words by characters in a script.

3. <u>Scene Heading/Slug line</u>: Describes the location and time of day for a scene.

4. <u>Character name</u>: Identifies which character is speaking or acting in a scene.

5. <u>Shot</u>: Describes how a scene is framed or filmed.

6. <u>Montage</u>: A sequence of short shots edited together to condense time or information.

7. <u>Voiceover (VO)</u>: Narration that is heard, but the character is not seen speaking on screen.

8. <u>Flashback</u>: A scene that interrupts the chronological flow of the main story to depict something that happened in the past.

Use these sparingly, you don't want to confuse your reader. Good writing does not involve a lot of "flashbacks."

9. <u>Climax</u>: The high point of the story where the conflict reaches its peak. Now this word won't appear in the script but you need to know and understand it's meaning.

10. <u>Denouement</u>: The resolution or outcome of the story that follows the climax.

These terms are essential for writers, directors, and other filmmakers to effectively communicate the visual and narrative elements of a script.

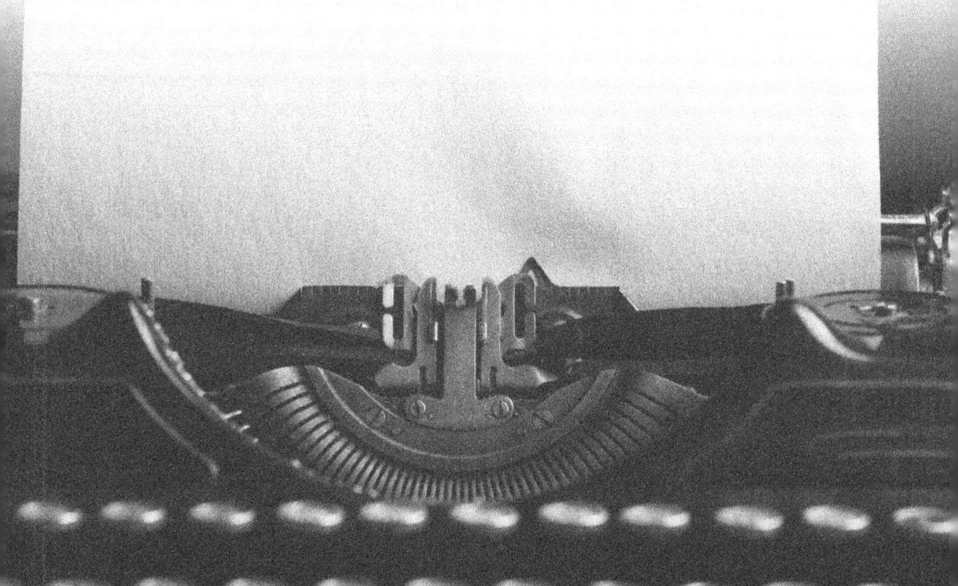

CHAPTER 8

WHY ARE THE FIRST TEN PAGES SO IMPORTANT?

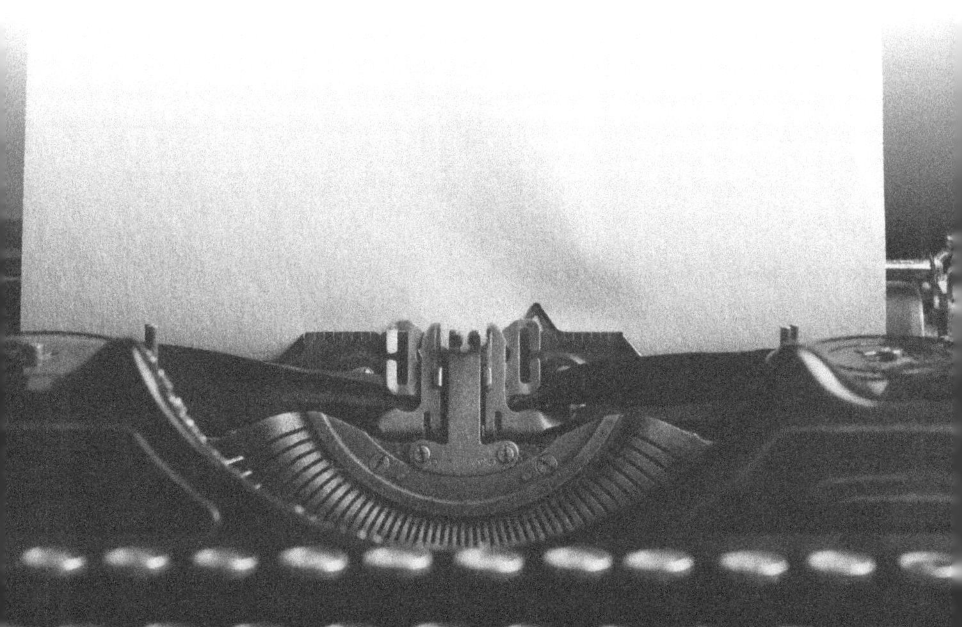

The first ten pages of a script are crucial because they serve as the foundation for the entire story and play a significant role in capturing the reader's (or audience's) attention.

HERE ARE SEVERAL REASONS WHY THE FIRST TEN PAGES ARE SO IMPORTANT IN A SCRIPT:

1. **First impressions**: The first few pages set the tone and establish the overall feel of the script. They provide the reader with their initial impression of the story, characters, and writing/storytelling style.

2. **Hooking the reader**: The opening pages need to grab the reader's attention and make them want to keep reading. A strong opening can intrigue the reader and make them eager to see how the story unfolds.

3. **Establishing the world**: The beginning of the script introduces the world in which the story takes place, including the setting, time period, and atmosphere. It helps the reader

understand the context of the story.

4. **Introducing the characters**: The first ten pages typically introduce the main characters and give the reader a sense of who they are, what they want, and how they relate to each other.

5. **Setting up the conflict**: The initial pages should establish the central conflict or problem that the characters will face throughout the story. This conflict sets the stage for the narrative and drives the plot forward.

6. **Creating momentum**: A compelling start builds momentum and propels the story forward. It sets the pace for the rest of the script and keeps the reader engaged.

7. **Establishing the genre and tone**:

The opening pages help establish the genre and tone of the script, whether it's a comedy, drama, thriller, or other genre. This informs the reader about what to expect from the story.

8. **Showing your writing skills**: The first ten pages are an opportunity to showcase your writing skills, creativity, and ability to craft a captivating story. It's your chance to make a strong impression on the reader.

Overall, the first ten pages of a script are critical for drawing in the reader, setting up the story, and laying the groundwork for the narrative to unfold. A strong start can make a script more compelling and increase its chances of capturing the interest of producers, directors, and audiences. Here is a list of top movies that have amazing first ten pages:

1. INCEPTION
2. The Piano
3. Portrait of a Lady on Fire
4. Promising Young Woman
5. Mudbound

6. Sunset Boulevard
7. Judas and the Black Messiah
8. The Invisible Man (2020)
9. American Beauty
10. Deadpool
11. Shaun of the Dead
12. Inglourious Basterds
13. Pulp Fiction

As a screenwriter, your first ten pages can make or break you in real life. Now, I personally think I've mastered the craft of "the first ten pages," but that is definitely subjective. Every screenwriting contest I've entered has told me that they loved the first ten pages. And honestly, most directors and producers will not read past those pages if they are not inspired. So, show them what you are working with and give them your very best in those pages.

I tend to treat the first ten as a mini movie. It has a beginning, a middle, and an end. I don't leave anything to surprise; I wow the reader with those first ten pages as if that is all I have for the story. I know that if they do not make it past the first ten, they have a great idea of my plot, main characters, and even potentially the conflict. So, treat these pages like its own full story. This will keep it interesting from beginning to end while preparing the reader for what is to come.

Chapter 9

SCRIPT OUTLINE

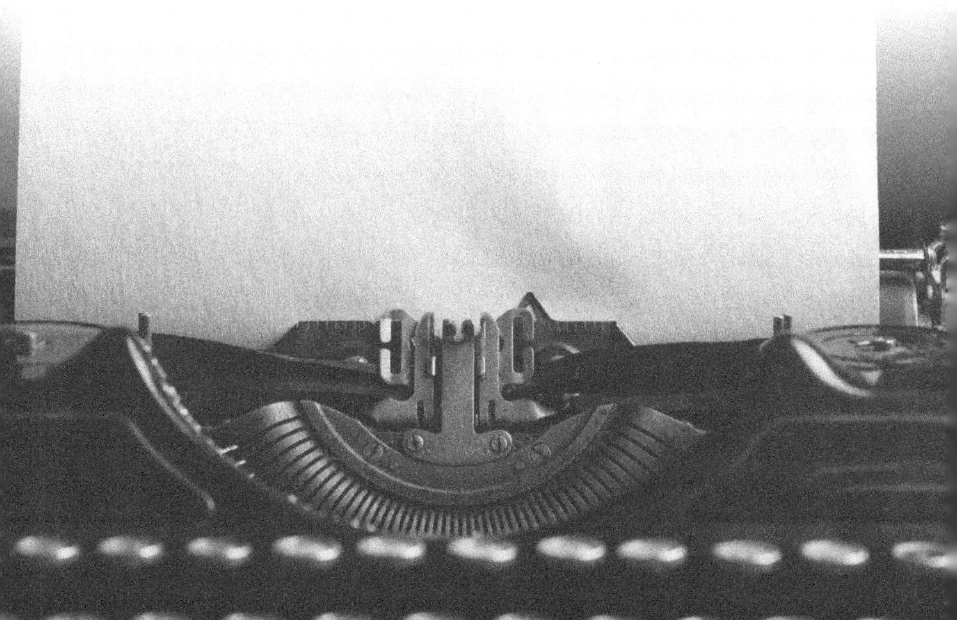

I know we've gotten so far into this book, covering so much information to get you started on this screenwriting journey. But it is safe to say, we have officially arrived at the starting line of your 31 day process!

While this next step isn't directly related to writing the script, it is crucial to your story planning and writing process. Make an outline. Now, to be honest, I didn't do this with my first few scripts and my writing suffered. Completely hashing out the story and addressing any confusing parts before you sit down and dedicate this month to your writing will save you so much time and lots of headaches after Act 3 ends.

CREATING AN OUTLINE FOR A SCRIPT IS CRUCIAL FOR SEVERAL REASONS:

1. **Structuring the story**: An outline helps you organize the plot, characters, and key events in a logical sequence. It allows you to see the big picture of your story and ensure

that the narrative flows smoothly from beginning to end.

2. **Clarifying the plot**: By outlining the major plot points and story beats, you can identify any inconsistencies, plot holes, or areas that need further development. This helps you refine the story and ensure that it is coherent and engaging.

3. **Developing characters**: An outline allows you to plan the character arcs, motivations, and relationships in advance. This helps you create well-rounded and compelling characters that drive the story forward.

4. **Maintaining focus**: With an outline, you can stay focused on the core elements of your story and avoid getting sidetracked by unnecessary

subplots or tangents. It serves as a roadmap to keep you on track with the main narrative.

5. **Saving time and effort**: Investing time in creating a detailed outline can save you time and effort during the writing process. It provides a clear roadmap for writing the script and helps you avoid getting stuck or potentially experiencing writer's block.

6. **Testing ideas**: An outline allows you to experiment with different story concepts, plot twists, and character developments before committing them to the script. This can help you refine your ideas and make informed creative decisions.

8. **Improving pacing**: By outlining the story's structure and pacing, you can ensure that the script has a balanced rhythm and builds tension effectively. This helps maintain the audience's engagement throughout the story.

In summary, an outline is a valuable tool that helps you plan, organize, and refine your script before diving into the actual writing process. It serves as a roadmap that guides you through the storytelling journey and ensures that your script is well-structured, cohesive, and compelling.

You know, a story essentially boils down to "who wants what, what's stopping them, and what do they do to get it?" and your outline does just that… outline these factors so you can write a complete story - a complete script - with confidence.

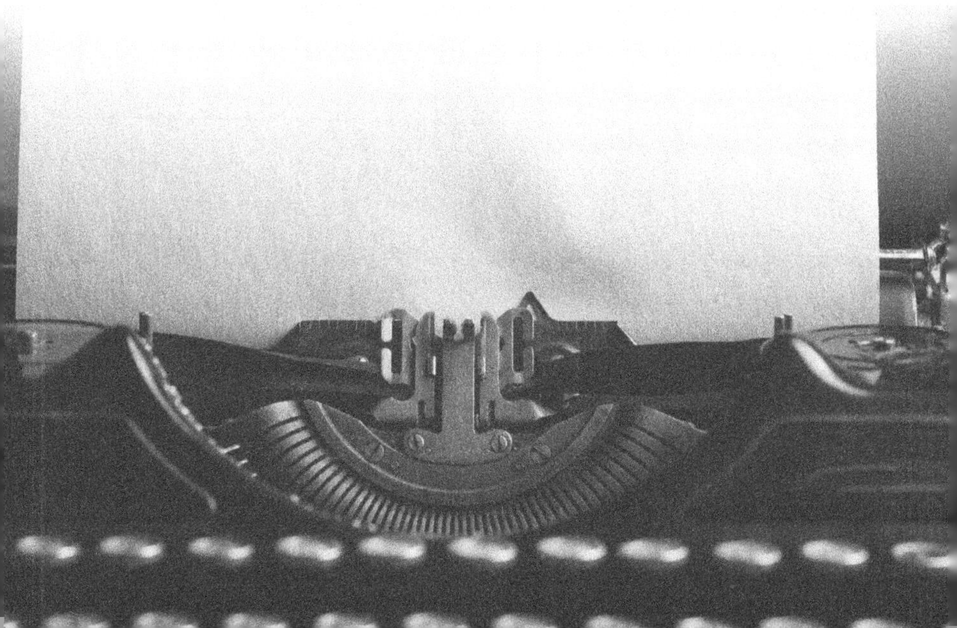

IN VERY SIMPLE TERMS, IT WOULD GO SOMETHING LIKE THIS:

THIS "TYPE OF PERSON"__________.

IS SUDDENLY CONFRONTED WITH THIS PROBLEM (OR OPPORTUNITY) _________.

AND MUST DEAL WITH IT OR ELSE __________.

SO, HE DECIDES TO_______, EVEN THOUGH HE'S UP AGAINST __________.

HE THEN PURSUES THAT GOAL ACTIVELY AND CONSISTENTLY DESPITE ONGOING AND ESCALATING OPPOSITION.

WHAT HE EXPERIENCES ALSO CHALLENGES THE CHARACTER'S DEFINING CHARACTERISTIC OF _______.

UNTIL IT BECOMES IMPOSSIBLE TO IGNORE THE REALIZATION__________.

AND THE CHARACTER RE-COMMITS TO HIS GOAL...

EMPLOYING NEW STRATEGIES AND INFORMED BY HIS NEW KNOWLEDGE, UNTIL HE ACHIEVES RESOLUTION.

You can use this as a rough template for your own outline. Of course, the more detailed and descriptive you are, the better your outline will be.

Howard Clay Jr.

CHAPTER 10

FIX YOUR DIALOGUE!

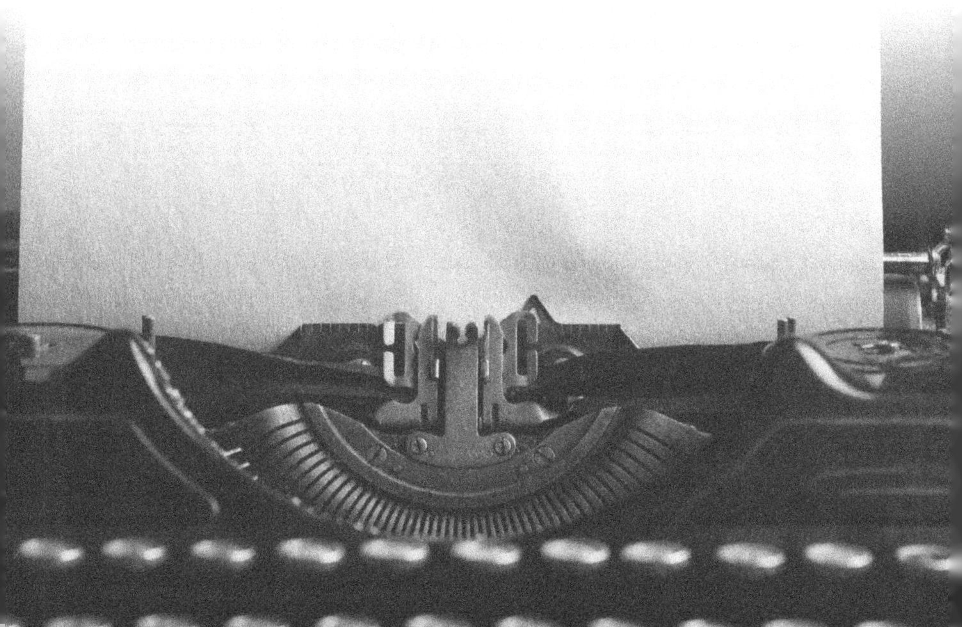

Before you writing another word or even before you write your first page of script, I want to talk about something that is very important and sometimes overlooked by a lot of screenwriters.

DIALOGUE.

Dialogue is so important and often overlooked when writing shorts, full scripts, or even television shows, but it can make or break your script in so many different ways. If I can help it, I don't want you to type one single word in your script until you understand the difference between dialogue and our own regular, everyday conversations.

DIALOGUE IN A SCRIPT DIFFERS FROM A LIVE CONVERSATION IN SEVERAL KEY WAYS. HERE ARE SOME OF THE MAIN DIFFERENCES:

1. **Purposeful**: Dialogue in a script is purposeful and serves to advance the story, reveal character traits, convey emotions, or provide important information to the audience. Every line of dialogue is carefully crafted

to serve a specific narrative or character-driven purpose.

2. **Concise**: Dialogue in a script is often more concise and to the point compared to natural conversation. Screenwriters aim to communicate information effectively within a limited space and time, so unnecessary small talk or filler is usually omitted.

3. **Subtext**: Good dialogue in a script often contains subtext - underlying meanings, emotions, or intentions that are not explicitly stated. Characters may say one thing but mean another, adding depth and complexity to the interaction.

4. **Structure**: Dialogue in a script follows a structured format, with each character's lines clearly labeled

and formatted according to industry standards. This structure helps actors, directors, and other members of the production team understand how the dialogue fits into the overall script.

5. **Conflict**: Dialogue in a script often involves conflict or tension between characters, as this helps drive the story forward and creates engaging scenes. Conflict can be verbal, emotional, or even physical, adding dramatic tension to the dialogue.

6. **Character consistency**: Dialogue in a script should be consistent with each character's personality, background, and motivations. Each character should have a distinct voice and way of speaking that reflects who they are and how they interact with others.

7. **Visual cues**: In a script, dialogue is often accompanied by visual cues, such as descriptions of character actions, reactions, or the setting. These cues help provide context and enhance the reader's understanding

of how the dialogue is meant to be performed on screen.

8. **Relevance**: Dialogue in a script is focused on what is relevant to the story being told. Unlike real-life conversations that may meander or include unrelated topics, dialogue in a script is purposeful and directly ties into the narrative.

Overall, the primary goal of dialogue in a script is to effectively convey information, develop characters, and propel the story forward in a way that engages the audience and enhances the overall viewing experience.

What I usually tell new writers is to start from the end of the conversation. Don't tell me that someone is "angry," but SHOW me someone angry. This is a script. You want as many visuals as possible. So, instead of saying that he was angry, say that he threw the glass across the room in rage. Create a visual with your words. The scene, actions, and character descriptions should be as detailed as possible for the reader. Another example would be if a character is nervous, write that they lost their wording or began stuttering. Bring the script to life with visuals, especially in the dialogue. It heightens the scene and makes it more interesting.

CHAPTER 10.5
CHARACTER ARCS

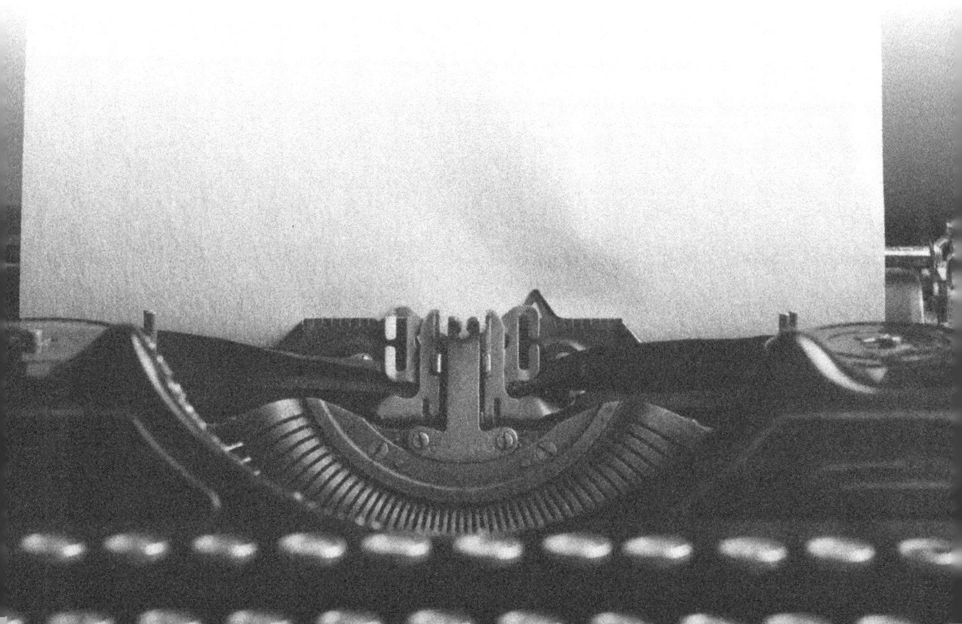

Take this next part with a grain of
salt because I believe creating and
building character acs is, by far, the
hardest thing to create in a script.
Other screenwriters may say something
different, so this is subjective.

Normally, I only focus on creating one
do it for the protagonist in the first
draft, then in my rewrite I work on the
antagonist's arc. This is my personal
recommendation, but you do what feels
right for you and your writing process.
Now, the good writers will give arcs
to each main character. But for
beginners, I suggest just building an
arc for the protagonist and antagonist
to start. Once you feel you have
mastered creating captivating arcs for
these characters, feel free to build
on your other supporting characters in
your rewrites. I'm not saying it is
impossible to do in the first draft,
I just don't think it's necessary to
focus on the arcs of each character
your first time through.

The character arc is an essential

element in storytelling, including
scripts, as it adds depth, complexity,
and emotional resonance to the
characters and the overall narrative.

HERE ARE SEVERAL REASONS WHY CHARACTER ARCS ARE
IMPORTANT IN A SCRIPT:

1. **Emotional Engagement**: A well-
developed character arc can evoke
emotions and empathy from the audience.
Seeing a character undergo growth,
change, and transformation can create a
powerful emotional connection between
the audience and the story.

2. **Character Development**: Character
arcs allow characters to evolve and
change over the course of the story.
This development can make characters
more relatable, interesting, and
dynamic, adding layers to their
personalities.

3. **Conflict and Tension**: Character arcs often involve internal conflicts, struggles, and challenges that characters must overcome. These obstacles create tension and drive the narrative forward, keeping the audience engaged and invested in the character's journey.

4. **Themes and Messages**: Character arcs can support the themes and messages of the story. Through the transformation of characters, the script can explore important themes such as redemption, forgiveness, love, or self-discovery in a meaningful way.

5. **Audience Satisfaction**: A satisfying character arc can provide a sense of closure and fulfillment for the audience. Watching a character grow, learn, and change can be rewarding for viewers and leave a lasting impact.

6. **Character Motivations**: Character arcs help to establish and clarify the motivations and actions of characters.

By understanding a character's growth and transformation, the audience can better comprehend their decisions and behaviors throughout the story.

In summary, character arcs play a crucial role in engaging the audience, developing characters, driving the narrative, conveying themes, and ultimately creating a memorable and impactful story.

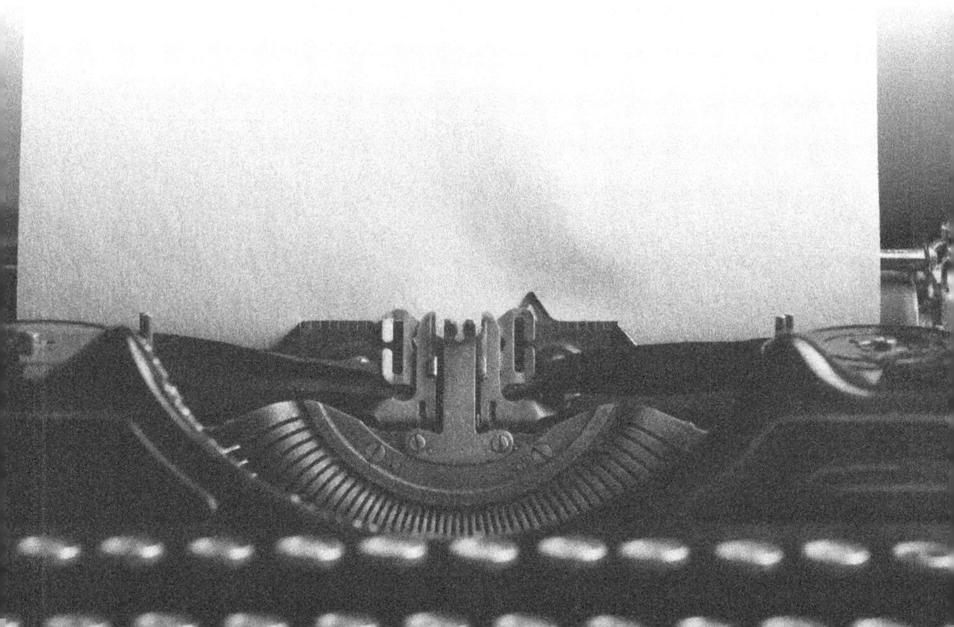

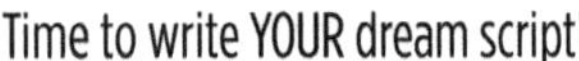 Time to write YOUR dream script!

CHAPTER 11
TIME TO WRITE YOUR DREAM SCRIPT

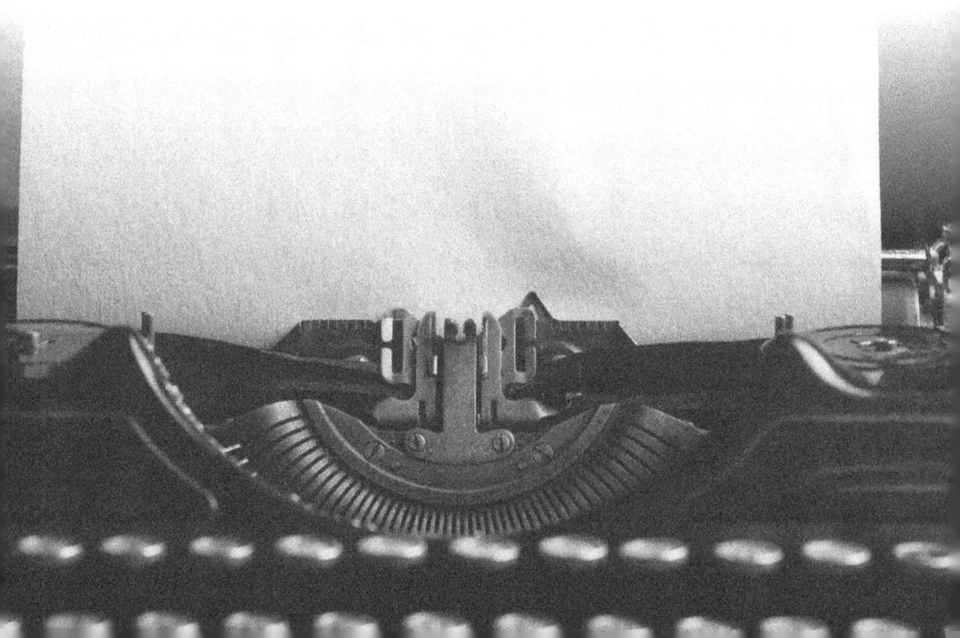

Over the next 31 days, I want you to write like you have never written before! Your goal is 90 pages. The reason I want you to start off with 90 pages is because I don't want you to get caught up in your own mind when it comes to telling your story. A lot of creators get lost in the details and it is hard for them to get out of it. Use the 90 pages like a therapy session where you get to word-vomit all over the page. Tell your story and don't stop until you are done.

Spend the first 30 pages of your script setting up the story. Pages 31-60 should focus on the conflict. The final 30 pages should deal with the solution. This is all general and relative based on your story. However, stick to ~30-page acts (remember, beginning, middle, and end) to help alleviate some of the pressure of trying to figure out this formula.

Just FYI, the standard length of a feature film script is typically around 90 to 120 pages, with many scripts falling in the 90-110 page range.

THERE ARE SEVERAL REASONS WHY A GOOD SCRIPT IS OFTEN AROUND 90 PAGES:

1. **Pacing**: A 90-page script generally translates to a runtime of about 90 minutes on screen, which is a common length for many feature films. This runtime allows for a well-paced story that keeps the audience engaged without dragging on or feeling rushed.

2. **Economy of storytelling**: A shorter script forces the writer to be more economical with their storytelling, focusing on the essential elements of the plot, character development, and themes. This can lead to a tighter, more focused narrative that avoids unnecessary filler or exposition.

3. **Budget constraints**: Shorter scripts are often more attractive to filmmakers and producers working with limited budgets, as they typically require fewer shooting days and resources to produce. This can increase the script's chances of being picked up for production.

4. **Audience engagement**: Keeping the script around 90 pages can help maintain the audience's attention and interest throughout the film. A concise script with a well-defined structure and compelling story beats is more likely to hold the viewer's focus from beginning to end.

5. **Commercial viability**: Many film festivals, competitions, and production companies have guidelines specifying a preferred script length, often falling within the 90-page range. Adhering to these standards can increase the script's marketability and potential for success in the industry.

6. **Industry standards**: The 90-page length has become a standard in the

film industry, making it easier for agents, producers, and other industry professionals to quickly assess the script's potential and feasibility for production.

While a good script can certainly vary in length, depending on the genre, style, and specific requirements of the story being told, aiming for around 90 pages can help ensure a well-structured, engaging screenplay that is more likely to resonate with readers, filmmakers, and audiences.

After you complete your 90 pages, we can get to the good part! Your first revision! 90 pages is short and sweet and hopefully will not be overwhelming once you reach the revision stages, helping you be even more successful as you continue through this process.

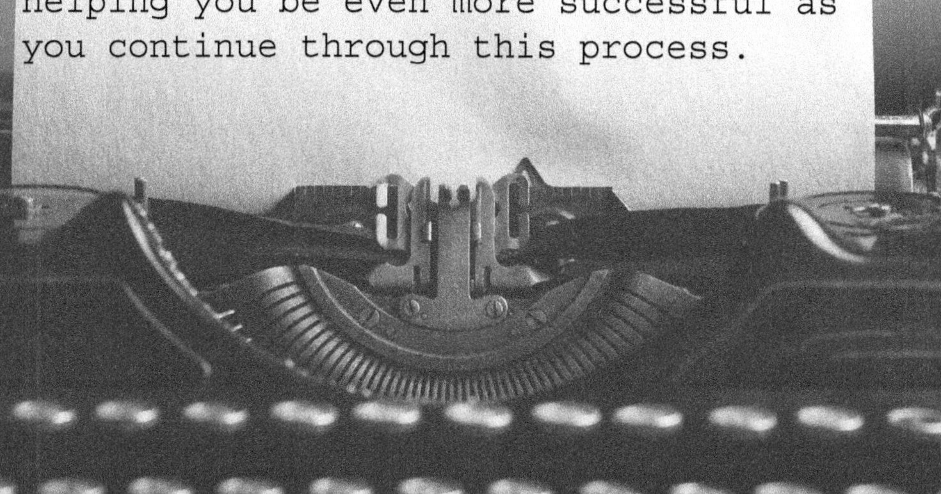

CHAPTER 12
1ST DRAFT EDIT

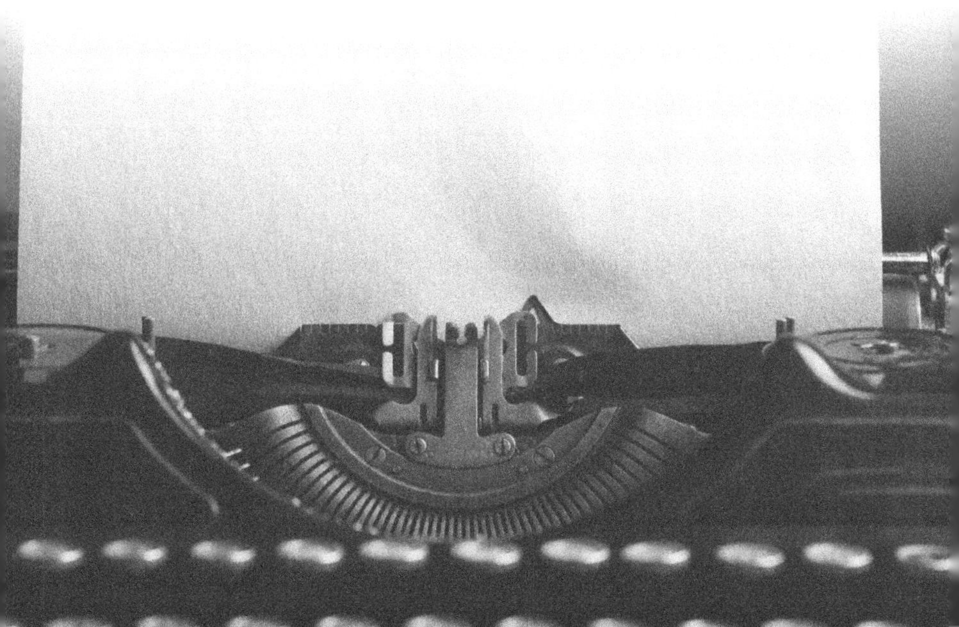

Editing is a major step in the scriptwriting process to refine and polish your work before sharing it with others or submitting it for production.

HERE ARE SOME STEPS YOU CAN FOLLOW TO EFFECTIVELY EDIT YOUR SCRIPT:

1. **Take a break**: After completing your script, give yourself some time away from it. This break will help you approach the editing process with fresh eyes and a clear perspective.

2. **Read your script aloud**: Reading your script out loud can help you identify awkward phrasing, dialogue that doesn't flow naturally, or pacing issues. It can also help you hear how the dialogue sounds and ensure that it rings true for the characters.

3. **Focus on structure**: Check the overall structure of your script, including the pacing, plot progression, character arcs, and thematic consistency. Make sure that each scene serves a purpose and contributes to the overall story.

4. **Cut unnecessary elements**: Identify any scenes, dialogue, or descriptions that do not contribute to the story or character development. Cut out any unnecessary or redundant elements to streamline your script.

5. **Check for continuity**: Ensure that there are no inconsistencies in the plot, character actions, or dialogue. Check for continuity errors and make sure that the story flows logically from beginning to end.

6. **Refine dialogue**: Pay close attention to your dialogue and make sure it sounds natural and authentic for each character. Remove any on-the-nose dialogue and consider adding subtext or layers of meaning to enhance the interactions.

7. **Proofread for grammar and spelling**: Carefully proofread your script for grammatical errors, spelling mistakes, punctuation issues, and formatting inconsistencies. A polished script demonstrates professionalism and attention to detail.

8. **Seek feedback**: Share your script with trusted friends, writing partners, or fellow writers for feedback. Consider joining a writing group or workshop to receive constructive criticism and suggestions for improvement.

9. **Revise and rewrite**: Based on feedback and your own observations, revise and rewrite sections of your script as needed. Be open to making changes that strengthen the story and improve the overall quality of the script.

10. **Final review**: Conduct a final review of your script to ensure that all edits have been implemented and that the script is in its best possible shape before sharing it with others.

By following these steps and approaching the editing process systematically, you can enhance the quality of your script and increase its chances of resonating with readers, filmmakers, and audiences.

As mentioned in earlier chapters, this would also be a good time to develop those character arcs for supporting characters. Adding additional characteristics into the script helps to make it pop and draw the interest of the reader. The devil is in the details and your first edit is where that process can begin.

If you've reached the editing phase, congratulations! You've finished your first script and I don't want to gloss over that without giving you some praise. I'm proud of you. Make sure you

post your success and tag me!

CHAPTER 13

SHOULD I SELL MY SCRIPT?

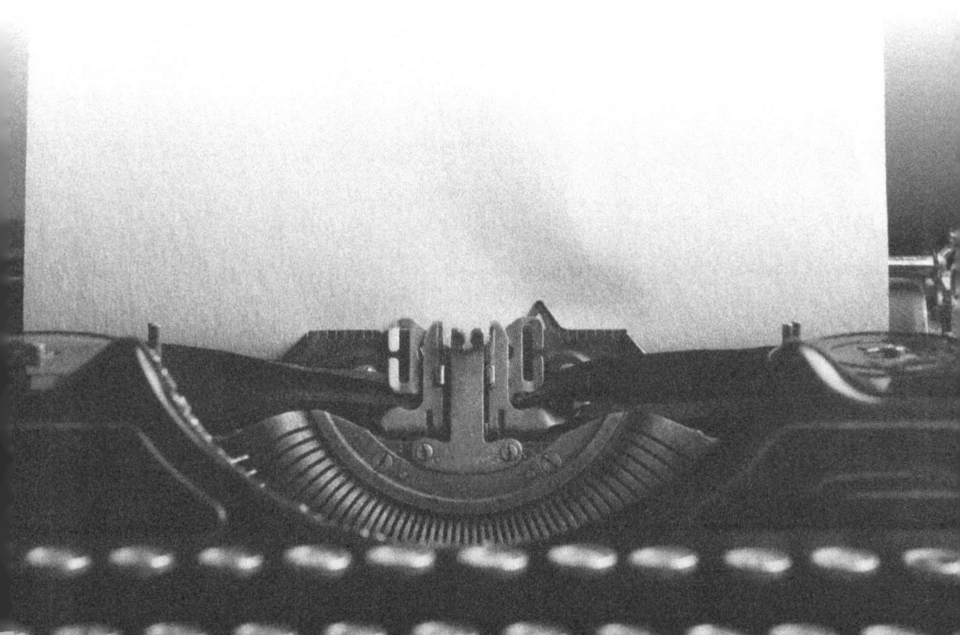

Selling a script can be a challenging task, but there are several ways you can increase your chances of success.

HERE ARE THE TOP 5 WAYS TO SELL YOUR SCRIPT:

1. **Script Competitions**: Submitting your script to reputable screenwriting competitions can provide exposure and recognition for your work. Winning or placing in a competition can attract the attention of industry professionals, agents, and producers.

2. **Script Query Letters**: Sending query letters to agents, managers, and production companies can help you get your script in front of industry professionals. Make sure your query letter is well-crafted and highlights the unique aspects of your script.

3. **Networking**: Building relationships with industry professionals through networking events, film festivals, and online platforms can help you connect with potential buyers for your script. Attend industry events, join screenwriting groups, and engage with

professionals on social media.

I have to pause and drop a gem right here… I used to be against going to festivals. But honestly, that is where I made the biggest connections. Do your research and have something ready to present or pitch. You never know who you will meet at a booth or in the lobby. Don't go to a festival with basic ideas; have something tangible you can leave with the people you meet, like a "one pager."

In my next book, How to Sell your Movie/TV Show in 31 Days, I will go into more detail about these types of events. But, for now, go and network. Just make sure someone there leaves interested in your work.

4. __**Hiring a Literary Agent**__: A literary agent can help you navigate the industry, pitch your script to the right people, and negotiate deals on your behalf. Look for reputable literary agents who specialize in your genre or type of script.
Getting a lit agent is harder than it looks! My suggestion would be to win a screenwriting competition to garner some buzz around you and your work. The competition may directly connect you with an agent.

5. **Pitching Your Script**: Attend pitch events, pitch fests, or pitch directly to production companies and studios (with the help of your agent or the people you have already connected with). Develop a compelling pitch that highlights the unique selling points of your script and practice delivering it effectively.

Remember, that selling a script often requires persistence, patience, and a willingness to revise and improve your work based on feedback. Good luck with selling your script!

Howard Clay Jr.

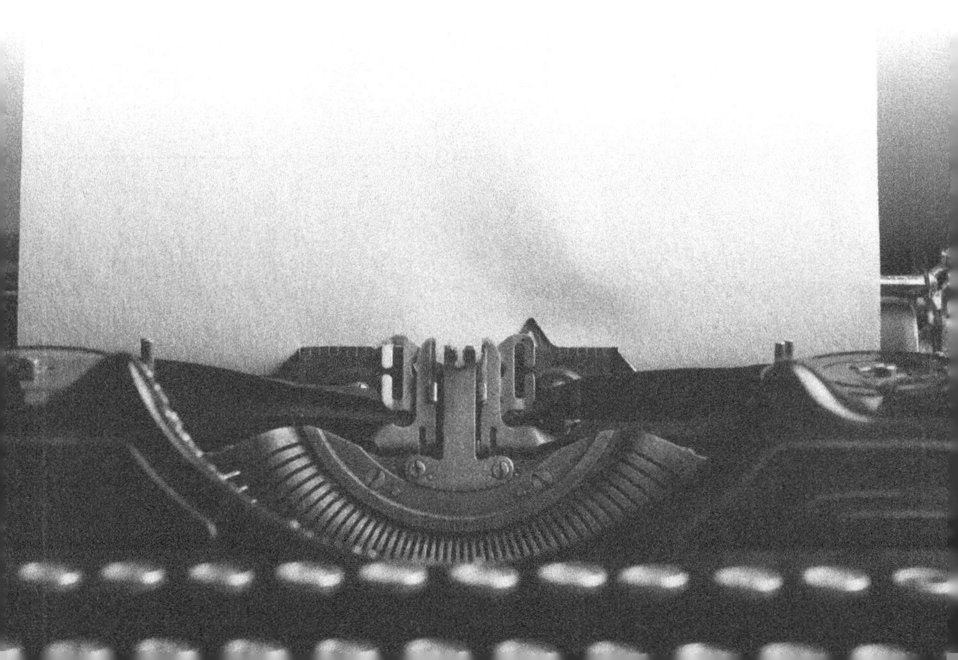

CHAPTER 14
SHOULD I PRODUCE MY OWN SCRIPT?

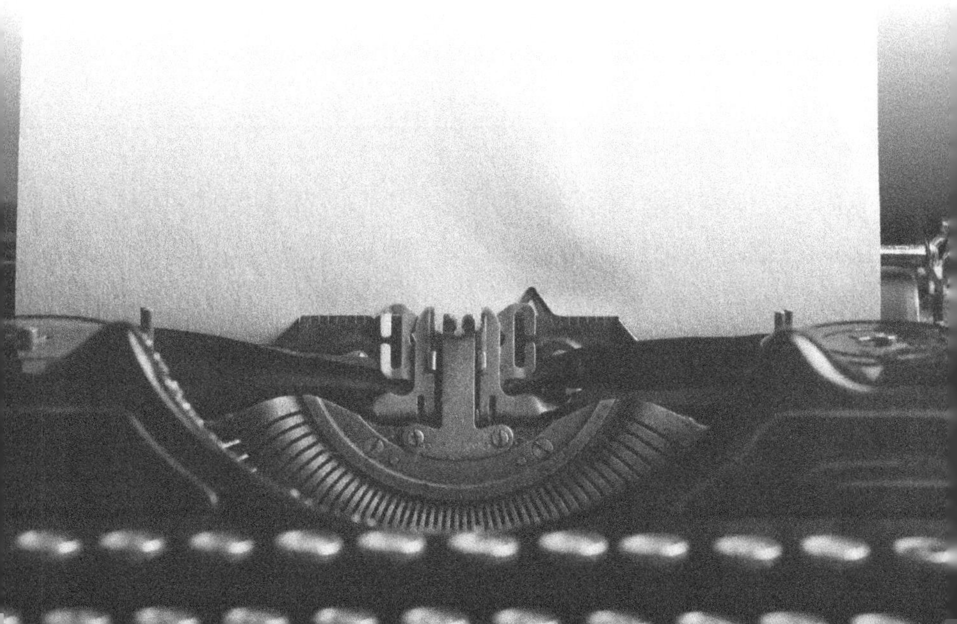

Producing your own script can be a rewarding and challenging endeavor.

HERE ARE THE TOP 5 REASONS WHY YOU MIGHT CONSIDER PRODUCING YOUR OWN SCRIPT:

1. **Creative Control**: As the producer of your own script, you have full creative control over the project. You can ensure that your vision is realized on screen without compromise.

2. **Showcase Your Talent**: Producing your own script can be a great way to showcase your writing and storytelling skills. It allows you to demonstrate your abilities as a writer, producer, and potentially, director.

3. **Investment in Your Career**: Producing your own script can serve as an investment in your career. It can help you build a portfolio of work, gain experience in the industry, and establish a track record as a filmmaker.

4. **Control Over Budget and Resources**: By producing your own

script, you have control over the budget, resources, and production schedule. You can make decisions based on your vision for the project and manage resources efficiently.

5. **Ownership and Rights**: Producing your own script allows you to retain ownership of the project and its rights. This can give you more control over how the project is distributed, marketed, and potentially lead to future opportunities for your work.

While producing your own script can be a fulfilling experience, it also comes with its own set of challenges and responsibilities. Make sure to carefully plan and prepare for the production process to maximize your chances of success.

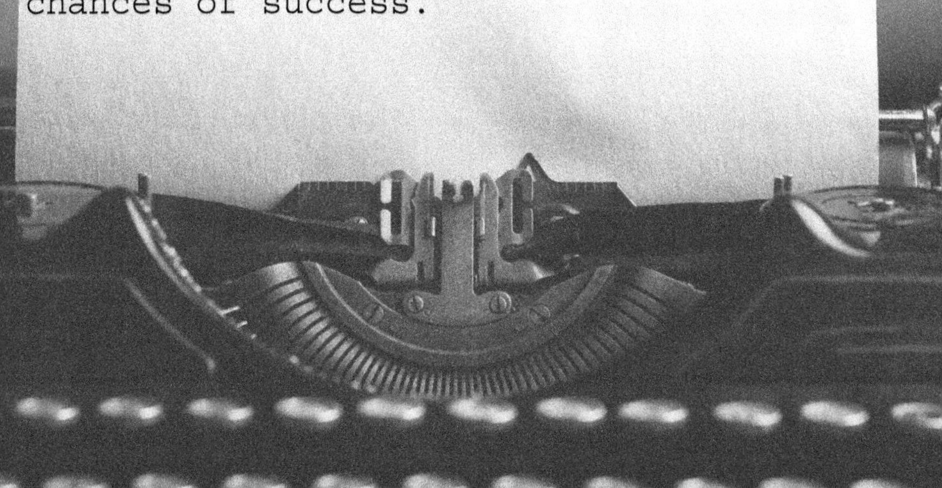

When I started out, I only wanted to be a screenwriter. I wanted to get to Hollywood and work in the writer's room. I had no idea what was in front of me. Producing my movie MILE 19 (currently on Peacock), was the greatest endeavor I could have achieved at this point. Is it an amazing movie? No, not at all. But, it is complete! Going through the process trained me in a lot of areas people are unfamiliar with.

Producing shorts is also another great way to learn what it takes to be a filmmaker. Making your own movie will mature you in this business. You will learn your strengths and weaknesses very quickly and you will hone your skills and talents. This is what will make you a filmmaker.

As we come to an end, let me close by saying, you are amazing, you are more than enough, and you are already a screenwriter before you finish your first script. Hopefully I've given you the tools to accomplish your goals. And as always, work hard, work smart, and ***I'LL SEE YOU AT THE MOVIES.***

THE END

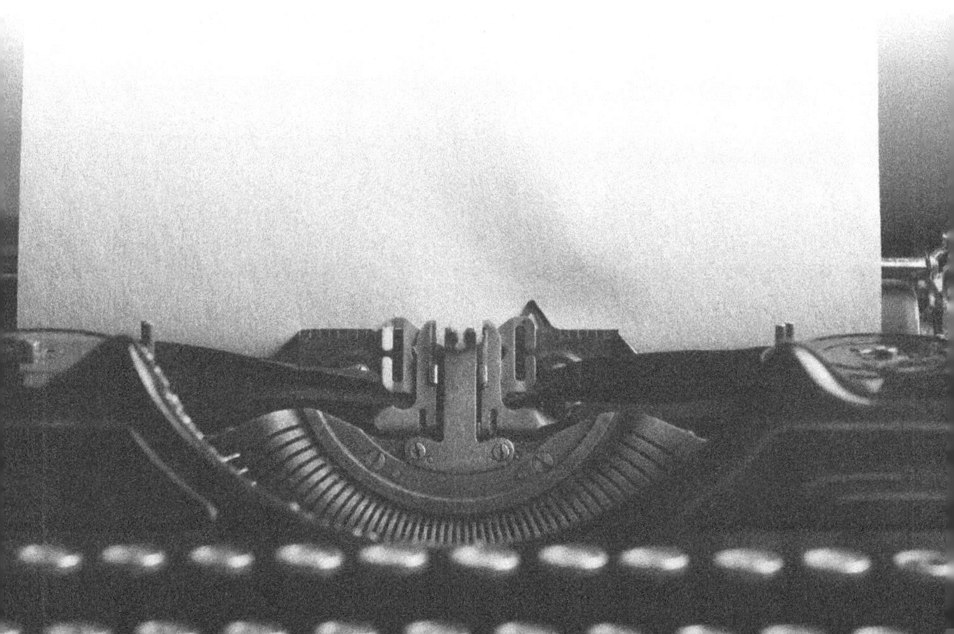